Passing the Tests

of Life

ISBN:978-1-950252-04-6

"Scripture taken from the New King James Version. Copyright © 1982 by
Thomas Nelson, Inc.

Passing the Tests of Life

By Summer McClellan

Other books by Summer McClellan

The Impossible Marriage

Grace, What is It?

Faith, What is It

Hope, What is It?

Broken Hearts

Satan Has No Power Over You

Jesus is Our Example

Light and Darkness

Dreams a Window to the Unseen

Love, What is It?

What Can I Do for God?

Contents

To my son,

James Aaron McClellan Jr.

Foreword

Many people who appear to "have it all" really have nothing and many people who appear to have nothing really "have it all."

It has always fascinated me to read about people's lives. I also like watching those biography shows on television. I have watched oodles of them. Watching the way other people have lived their lives is a real learning experience.

Famous people, in particular, have always fascinated me, probably because I have felt so very unsuccessful and insignificant, especially financially, but in many other ways as well. I absolutely could not imagine what it would be like to be rich, famous, beautiful and successful, like the people on television and movies. The people we are taught by our society have "made it."

But I learned a lot watching all those biographies and reading all those life stories. Many of those people were miserable. In a way they were failures and their lives ended in tragedy. Many have died young alone and miserable leaving behind a trail of wounded lives behind them. Some died of drug overdoses, some from suicide, some went crazy, and many died completely alone. Some went from marriage to marriage, ruining the lives of their children. How could those with fame and the money and everything that goes with it not have happy lives? Could it be they failed the tests of life? That the things they attained left them empty.

And there are also those with moral failures who let their lusts consume them. That even though they achieved a measure of success, their sexual lusts brought them down. A small part of life, sex, consumed the rest of their life canceling out their successes.

And many of the rich and powerful industrial giants who had lust for great wealth but viewed human lives as expendable, just a means to put them on the top, they don't impress me. Factory conditions were unsafe, workdays were long, and wages were a pittance. Men died easily. Were these rich moguls really on the top? Or was every life they wasted for their own greed digging them deeper into the pit? Sometimes what looks like up in our world is really down in eternity? These super wealthy made their whole lives about wealth and power, but at the expense of the souls of men.

There have been so many men and women who have looked successful but for some reason or another have miserably failed the tests of life.

Of course, all of us have failed in some areas of our

lives. The Bible is very honest about the successes and also the failures of our favorite Bible heroes. This is for our benefit. So, we can learn from them. Abraham, Moses, Joshua, Elijah, David and Solomon and of course many more who are all monumental to our faith, but they all have had their failures recorded also. Success and failure really will ultimately be between each soul and their Creator. Some who look successful have really failed miserably and some who look like failures were not, in God's eyes they have succeeded.

We are all being tested continually. These tests determine our destinies not just here on earth but eternally. The more we pass the higher we go.

Would you like to learn more about passing the tests of life? Please read on!

For what shall it profit a man if he shall gain the whole world and lose his own soul? Mark 8:36

Chapter One

Tests

*Each one's work will become manifest; for the Day will
declare it, because it will be revealed by fire; and the fire
will test each one's work, of which sort it is.*
1 Corinthians 3:13

There is a day coming when the things we have done in
this life will be tested. Our work will become manifest. In other
words, everything will be laid out on the table; the real truth
will be seen. What was our life about? Was it acceptable to
God? Did we pass the test of fire that shows up our true works,
our true motives? When your works are tested by fire what will
be revealed? This is it; this is the big test; will we pass?

We are continually going through tests. Some tests are
big, and some are small. Our life is filled with them. We are
continually being tested and tried. Some tests come from God
and some from the devil. It may seem unimportant to some to
pass the tests that are being given to us by the unseen realm.
But it is important, extremely important.

A Test in a Parking Lot

A friend of mine checked himself into an alcohol rehab
facility because the problem he had with alcohol had cropped
up again. He had a family, and his drinking was a huge issue. Not
just the drinking but also money, and the pinch his drinking
caused. Not long after he had successfully completed his alcohol

rehab, he went to the grocery store. Afterward, in the parking lot, as he rolled his cart back to the cart corral, he noticed something in the bottom of the last cart in the corral. It was a case of beer. Free beer, just sitting there. He froze. Normally this would be a dream come true. He had never had anything like that happen before. The thought hit him, "I'll just drink this free beer and never drink again." Suddenly he realized this was a test, a test from his enemy to get him drinking again. He turned and got out of there as fast as he could. He passed this test!

To pass the tests, in our lives, takes diligence on our part and to take things seriously. The good news is that passing tests leads to promotion. It leads to blessings and more authority. They lead to a higher level of living.

Tests are a matter of choices. Some tests are true and false questions, simple choices of right and wrong. Some tests are multiple choices; the right answer is in there somewhere.

The bottom line is you are being tested whether you like it or not. The things you do and say with your life, the choices you make it all adds up to the final grade and it makes a difference on whether you pass or fail in your life. Obviously to pass the test of your life you cannot just believe you are just some cosmic mistake, and nothing matters. No, just the opposite, everything matters because God exists, and your life is taken seriously and lived carefully to please Him.

Tests are a part of our life and there is no getting out of them. They begin when we are very small, and they continue on throughout our life on earth. Tests are determining our eternal position. God is testing us with the intention of promoting us and Satan is testing us with the intention of destroying us. We only need to look closely at a person's life and see the tests that are there, that they have faced or are facing.

Joseph, from the Bible, is one whose tests in his life stand out to me.

Joseph was Tested

My all-time favorite Bible character and a good example of a man, who passed the tests in his life, is the story of Joseph, written in Genesis. For those who haven't read Genesis you may have heard of him anyway, if you have seen the play *Joseph and the Amazing Technicolor Dream Coat.* Joseph's life is an incredible story.

Joseph was the favorite son of Jacob, a rich but godly man, who showers his favorite son with the coat of many colors, Joseph's famous coat. Joseph's ten older brothers were extremely jealous of Joseph. Not only is Joseph their father's favorite but Joseph bragged to them about the dreams he had; dreams play a huge role in Joseph's story. Joseph dreams of a field with sheaves of wheat, and his brothers' sheaves of wheat all come and bow down to his. Then he dreams of the sun, moon and eleven stars {his brothers} all bowing down to him. This only causes his brothers to hate him more.

They were all shepherds and when Joseph's father, Jacob, sent Joseph to find his brothers and the check on them, the brothers seized their opportunity and were going to kill their brother Joseph. Rather than kill him they changed their minds and sold him into slavery to some passing merchants. Then the brothers kill an animal and cover Joseph's beautiful coat with the blood. They bring the bloody coat to their father and convince him that

Joseph is dead. It nearly broke Jacob's heart with grief. Meanwhile the merchants then traveled to Egypt and sold Joseph, as a slave, to Potiphar, an officer of the Pharaoh, the ruler of Egypt.

This is where Joseph begins to show us his true character, and he begins passing tests. Joseph works hard as a slave. He does such a good job that his owner, Potiphar, puts him in charge of everything he owns. Joseph is soon running Potiphar's entire household.

This is amazing to me; I would think that Joseph would refuse to work and keep trying to escape and get back to his father. But he doesn't, he works hard as a slave.

His tests keep coming. Potiphar's wife tries to seduce him. Every day she tries to seduce him but every day he refuses her. Joseph is facing a big test here; he is being daily pursued by a beautiful woman. Many men would not have passed this one, but Joseph did.

Joseph has not been treated fairly; he has been ripped from his life and from his family by his own brothers and made a slave. But he has made the best of things and worked hard. I am sure at some point he has tried to tell someone he was unfairly sold as a slave and his father will pay for his return, but he is not rescued. Now he has a chance to get even with his master and sleep with his wife, but that is not his attitude at all. He answers her that it would be a sin against God.

Here is the key to his behavior. He is concerned how his life looks to God. He is not out for vengeance; he is living to please God. That is his secret to passing the tests that he is going through.

Next Potiphar's wife gets even with Joseph for refusing her; she tells her husband that Joseph tried to rape her. Joseph is treated unfairly again. Now, Potiphar throws Joseph into prison for something he didn't do. What could be worse? Even though Joseph lives to please God and behaves beyond reproach, his life gets even worse. And yet he still works hard. He doesn't get angry with God, and he doesn't get bitter. He continues to pass tests; he does his very best, even in prison. We are told in prison he works hard and is put in charge of the entire prison.

Joseph is an exceptional young man. I don't think I could have this attitude. I think I would have a pity party and sit in the corner of the prison cell and cry all day to God how unfair things were. But not Joseph, he is doing his very best whatever situation he is put in. He is passing tests.

As time goes on, Pharaoh's chief butler and chief baker are put in prison. One day they both are disturbed by dreams which they tell Joseph, and he interprets correctly. The butler's dream meant that in three days' time he would be restored to his position by the Pharaoh. The baker's dream meant that in three days he would be executed.

At this time Joseph asks the butler to speak to the Pharaoh for him when he is restored to his butler position. Joseph asks him to tell Pharaoh that he was stolen and sold into slavery and falsely imprisoned and to remember him and get him out of prison. Well, the baker was executed, and the butler was restored, just as Joseph had correctly predicted. But the butler forgot him. Joseph faces disappointment again.

Two long years later, the Pharaoh had a troubling dream. The Pharaoh called all his wise men and magicians, but no one could tell him what his dreams meant. Finally, the butler remembered Joseph and told the Pharaoh about Joseph and that he could interpret dreams. This is where the story gets good. Joseph was called out of the prison to stand before the Pharaoh. Joseph interprets Pharaoh's dreams, and the Pharaoh is so impressed with Joseph, he puts him in charge of the whole country; Joseph is second only to the Pharaoh. Wow talk about having a good day!

This is such a wonderful and amazing story for many reasons. One reason is that everything Joseph went through, being a slave and then being put in charge of his master's household and then being a prisoner and being put in charge of the entire prison, had prepared him to be in charge of the entire country of Egypt. He was continually being tested and passing his tests. His tests were not meaningless, they were designed for him, and they were perfect training. Joseph had been chosen by God for an important position and by passing his tests Joseph proved worthy of it. I have heard that it was about thirteen years before he was made ruler of Egypt, which is a long time to suffer.

Eventually Joseph is reunited with his family. But what I want to mention is that Joseph continues a life that is pleasing to God. Wouldn't you think that Joseph would have a list of people to get even with? All those years of suffering wouldn't you think he would be planning revenge? Let's see, there were his brothers, the merchants that sold him to Potiphar and then Potiphar and his stupid wife. Joseph could have clicked his fingers and had them all thrown into prison. And there was even the butler who let him sit in jail another two years.

But that was not his attitude at all. Here are the words he spoke to his brothers in Genesis 50:20-21 *"But as for you, you meant evil against me; but God meant it for good, in order to bring it about as it is this day, to save many people alive. Now therefore do not be afraid; I will provide for you and your little ones." And he comforted them and spoke kindly to them.*

Joseph has completely forgiven his brothers and actually supports them. He is the kind of man a world leader should be, not only in this life but especially in the life to come, eternal life. He got there by-passing tests. He passed the test of stewardship. He was faithful handling the affairs of Potiphar and the affairs of the prison he was put in. Even though he had been kidnapped from his father and sold as a slave he still was the best slave he could be. And then when bad got worse and Joseph was thrown into prison because of a lie, he still gave it his best.

Joseph passed other tests as well. He passed the test of sexual temptation. The Bible tells us Potiphar's wife tried to seduce Joseph, day after day. He was consistently facing temptation on a daily basis and yet he resisted. He passed this difficult test with flying colors.

Joseph also passed the test of patience. Joseph

spent many years in captivity but still he remained faithful to God. Joseph does not become weary in well doing; he consistently lives in an upright way after years of injustice. Joseph is faithful to pass every test that comes his way, even the test of success. When Joseph becomes the ruler of Egypt, he does not get even with his enemies. He did give his brothers a test of his own, but he loves and forgives them. He does not use his power to get revenge. Do you see why Joseph is one of my very favorite Bible characters? I love him!

Tests are coming into our lives. Whether or not we pass them is up to us. They are extremely important. They will decide our future, not only in this life but in eternity. Maybe you don't realize you are going through tests. You are, they are all around you, and you face them continually. You did not get where you are by mistake. Have you faced injustice, betrayal from those you love, mistreatment, disappointment and more? Like Joseph you can pass these tests, Joseph's secret was his unshakeable belief that what he did was important to God, and he chose to be faithful.

Chapter Two

Who is Watching You ?

And your Father who sees in secret will reward you openly.
Matthew 6:18b

I recently watched a popular television show, in which the host frequently helps people with their love lives. On this particular episode the host was helping a pretty young gal find the right man. She wanted someone with character, someone she could trust.

So, the host picked out four nice looking bachelors for her to choose from. Each one went separately on a date with her at the same restaurant. But what the men didn't know was that they were going to go through a character test. What looked like a restaurant full of people was really a carefully orchestrated test. There were hidden cameras recording their every move and the people around them were actors.

The first test each bachelor faced was when a man would get up and walk by their table and drop a twenty-dollar bill as he passed. Would the dates return it or keep it? Only one of the men returned the money.

There were other tests too. The pretty young gal

would excuse herself from the table and head to the bathroom. While she was gone an attractive waitress would come up and begin flirting with her date and try to give the current bachelor her phone number. All this was planned to see how the young men would respond. Three of them flirted back and took her phone number, only one declined. The one who declined even told the young lady about it when she returned to the table.

The next test was to see how they would help a person in distress. An older lady, really another actor, goes to pay her bill but her credit card is denied. She becomes very upset that she can't pay her bill, and everyone can hear her. The same young man who turned down the waitress paid her bill; he was the only one.

Live on the show now, was the young gal and the four dates. The four bachelors found out they had been watched on a hidden camera throughout the dates and their behavior had been tested. Most were quite embarrassed as they and everyone else watched the footage of their dates. They were realizing their poor behavior hadn't gone unnoticed and now not only was just the young gal that they were hoping to impress watching them, but also, a whole television audience. The three young men with the poor behavior were speechless. Seeing their behavior played back to them was painful.

After all the tests were watched, the television show host asked the young gal which young man she would choose to date and of course she picked the one who had behaved the best when no one was looking. He won the girl. The others would have behaved differently had they known they were being watched.

You are Being Watched

My point is this: you are always being watched! You will never do anything in secret! The physical realm, this natural world that we live in, is like a stage that is set before the spiritual realm and all there can see us. We are all like the four young men, we are constantly being tested. We need to decide now, to live our lives openly before God to please Him. Our actions, our words, our thoughts, our motives, all are laid bare before Him. But not only God can see us, that is only just the beginning we are also seen by angels, and of course the evil side. The devil and cohorts are watching us hoping we will fail. Also, the Bible tells us we are surrounded by a great cloud of witnesses, those who have gone before us. That is quite an audience. Will we be embarrassed like the bachelors were?

A Not So Secret Affair

I read a story an older pastor wrote about himself when he first got started. He was single back then, back in the late 1930's and praying for a wife. He traveled to different churches preaching and everyone had an idea who he should marry. There was a certain girl everyone had picked out for him; she seemed like a good fit.

One night while he was praying in his room, his spirit lifted out of his body. The Lord took him in the spirit up and out of his house, and down a certain street, a dark alley. There was a car parked there and his spirit went right into the car. There in the back seat of this car was the girl everyone had picked out for him. She was in the back seat engaging in an extra marital affair. He was only there for a minute and then his spirit was returned to his room. The Lord was revealing the character of this girl to him; she was not a suitable wife for the young minister. Of course, the pastor did not marry this girl.

Nothing is done in secret.

God's Reveals the Problem

My son found out when he was six years old, that nothing is done in secret. He was sitting in the living room with his new baby sister who was in the baby swing. I was in the kitchen washing dishes. Suddenly the baby started wailing. On my way into the living room the Lord showed me a picture. It was of a toothpick. I walked into the living room. There was my son trying to look innocent. I asked my son did he have a toothpick. He looked surprised and then opened his hand and handed it to me. He wanted to see what would happen if he poked the baby with a toothpick. There is no such thing as doing something unseen.

A Three-Year-Old Straightens Up

I had to laugh at a story told to me about my brother-in-law, Walter. When he was a three-year-old, he was a terror. He was in the living room and his mother was in the kitchen. She called to him to pick up his toys from the other room. He stuck out his tongue in the direction of his mother, knowing she couldn't see him from where he was. But what he didn't realize was that because of a mirror on the wall of the living room he was visible to her from the kitchen.

"I saw that", his mother called from the other room. Walter was shocked and couldn't figure out how she knew he had stuck out his tongue. For years he thought his mother could see everything he did. He behaved much better! We need to learn the lesson this three-year-old learned. We won't get away with anything!

We need to know our heavenly Father sees us in secret and we must live our lives for His eyes. Joseph did it. His life, although forgotten by everyone, was being watched by God and Joseph passed his tests. Remember, you are being watched.

Someone else, who is also invisible, is also watching us. The devil puts out temptation before us and he hopes we will bite. He is waiting for you to fail your tests so he can demand a legal right to any part of your life he can get. His ultimate goal is to steal your soul so he can make a legal claim on it when you die, and eternal torment follows. Nothing is worth this, nothing; we must begin to pass our tests, even the ones that don't come from God, the ones that come from Satan.

To close this chapter, I would like to end with a quote from the book, *God Calling*. It is a timeless classic that was written by two listeners who listen to Jesus and write His words to them.

No follower of mine would ever err or fall, if once the veil were withdrawn which prevents him from seeing

how these slips delight the evil spirits, and the pain and disappointment of those who long for him to conquer in My Strength and Name, and the ecstasy of rejoicing when victory is won.

We are being watched by, God, the angels and saints in heaven, also by the devil and his cohorts. Nothing we do is in secret, we are standing on the stage of eternity, there is an audience watching our life, and we are determining our own eternal destiny!

Chapter Three

The Most Important Test

"For what profit is it to a man if he gains the whole world, and loses his own soul?" Matthew 16:26

There are many tests that you will face in your life but the most important test of all is your salvation. It has one question. What will you do with Jesus? Will you accept the salvation He has provided for you when He stood in your place and took your sin so that you could be right with God? It is a simple yes or no answer. Do you enter eternity and stand before God covered with the righteousness of Christ Jesus, purchased by His blood, cleansed from sin because you answered "yes." Or, do you enter eternity naked, guilty, and unrighteous because you answered "no" or worse yet because you simply didn't answer?

It sounds so simple. Could it be that simple? Could something that simple really be important at all? I have noticed something about God. He doesn't make things complicated for us. All we have to do is say "yes" and follow one step at a time.

A Sorting is Coming

We read in the Bible about a sorting that is coming. There is a sorting of the wheat from the chaff. *His winnowing fan is in His hand, and He will thoroughly clean out His threshing floor, and gather His wheat into the barn; but he will burn up the chaff with unquenchable fire. Matthew 3:12*

We hear of the wheat in the chaff again in Matthew chapter 13:24-30 *Another parable He put forth to them, saying: "The kingdom of heaven is like a man who sowed good seed in his field; but while he slept, his enemy came and sowed tares among the wheat and went his way. But when the grain had sprouted and produced a crop, then the tares also appeared. So, the servant of the owner came and said to him, 'Sir, did you not sow good seed into your field? How the does it have tares?' He said to them, 'An enemy has done this.' The servants said to him,' Do you want us then to go and gather them up?' But he said, 'No lest you gather the tares you also uproot the wheat with them. Let both grow together until the harvest, and at the time of the harvest I will say to the reapers, "First gather the tares and bind them in bundles to burn them but gather the wheat into my barn.'"*

In verse 37-43 Jesus explains the parable. *He answered and said to them: "He who sows the good seed is the Son of Man. The field is the world, the good seeds are the sons of the kingdom, but the tares are the sons of the wicked one. The enemy who sowed them is the devil, the harvest is the end of the age, and the reapers are the angels. Therefore, as the tares are gathered and burned in the fire, so it will be at the end of this age. The Son of Man will send out His angels, and they will gather out of His kingdom all things that offend, and those who practice lawlessness, and will cast them into the furnace of fire. There will be wailing and gnashing of teeth. Then the righteous will shine forth as the sun in the kingdom of their Father. He who has ears let him hear."*

In verse 47 Jesus mentions the sorting again. *"Again, the kingdom of heaven is like a dragnet that was cast into the sea and gathered some of every kind, which when it was full, they drew to shore; and they sat down and gathered the good into vessels but threw the bad away. So, it will be at the end of the age. The angels will come forth, separate the wicked from the just, and cast them into the furnace of fire. There will be wailing and gnashing of teeth."*

Jesus mentions another sorting in Matthew 25, this time He is sorting the sheep from the goats. He tells us when He comes, He will gather the nations and He will separate them one from another as a shepherd divides the sheep from the goats. The goats are sent to everlasting punishment and the sheep to eternal life.

Each of us will be tested in this sorting process, there is no escaping it. Will we pass this test? There is only one way to pass it, through Jesus, covered in His righteousness, living For Him. Will you pass this test? What will you do with Jesus? Yes, or No?

Chapter Four

The Purpose of Tests

"He who is faithful in what is least is faithful also in much; and he who is unjust in what is least is unjust also in much. Therefore, if you have not been faithful in unrighteous mammon, who will commit to your trust the true riches? And if you have not been faithful in what is another man's, who will give you what is your own?" Luke 16:10-12

There have been many articles in our local paper and stories on our local news of people embezzling. It seems to be an epidemic. The woman at our local hospital in charge of soliciting donations embezzled a huge sum. Also, a local township secretary committed a similar crime. That was just the beginning there was a school principal, a nonprofit worker, a banker, a mother who was in charge of a children's sports fund, an office worker at a construction company, a health worker stealing from their elderly patient, etc. etc... And that is just in our area, the problem is all over the country. Americans have lost billions of dollars trusting investment companies who have been living it up on their money. The bottom line is untrustworthy people have been put in positions of authority that should not have been there. They have caused suffering and pain because of their evil actions. Some have even killed to cover up their fraud. All these people were put in positions of trust, positions to oversee the property of others. They failed their tests miserably.

Can You Be Trusted?

God is setting up an eternal kingdom. There are important positions to be filled, positions of honor and authority. Positions that are in a kingdom that never ends. God is testing you in every situation He puts you in. Can you be trusted? Can you be trusted with worldly wealth? Can you be trusted in the situation you are in? Can you even be trusted in small things?

One of the purposes for the tests in your life is to place you in a position, not only on earth but also in heaven. God is finding out if you can be trusted. If you can, He will entrust you with His power, with His authority and with spiritual gifts.

For instance, our words hold power. Can God trust you with your words? If He can, He can also increase the power of your words. If He can't trust your words, He will weaken the power behind your words.

Joseph Passed the Test

Joseph was severely tested for many years. It was extreme because of the position of authority God had planned for Joseph. Joseph was probably the most powerful man on the planet in his time. He had the food stored up and the people of the world came to him. Let's go back to Joseph's story.

Joseph was called out of prison by the Pharaoh because he had two dreams that terrified him. As Joseph stood before the Pharaoh, Pharaoh told Joseph the two dreams. He dreamed he saw seven fat healthy cows and then seven scrawny cows came and swallowed them up. Then Pharaoh dreamed of seven healthy heads of corn and then seven scraggly heads of corn swallowed them up. Joseph told the Pharaoh the meaning of the dreams; first there would be seven years of plenty coming and they would be followed by seven years of famine.

Joseph suggested to the Pharaoh that he store up food during the seven years of plenty for the seven lean years that would follow. The Pharaoh was so impressed with Joseph that he put Joseph in charge of this food project. He made him the highest ruler in the land, second only to Pharaoh.

Joseph was ready for the job. He had been in charge of Potiphar's house, and he had been in charge of the prison. In both he had proved faithful. Now he was in charge of Egypt. Joseph collected so much food during the seven years of plenty that it was beyond counting. Then the famine came. Not only did Joseph feed the people of Egypt; many people from many nations came to him for food. He saved the lives of multitudes, but most importantly to him was his own family. They came to Egypt during the famine looking for food. Joseph provided for them and saved their lives.

Joseph was literally the most powerful man in the world. Without him many, many people would have died. He was faithful in that position because he had passed his tests. He was living to please God.

Passing Tests Leads to Promotions

You will have many tests in your life. When you pass, you get promoted. Blessings follow tests. You move up to a new level. You gain more authority in your walk with God. Joseph had incredibly hard tests because of the high calling that he was called to. Joseph was promoted from an inmate in prison to a position of incredible authority.

Immediately, when Joseph was promoted by the Pharaoh, he was given the Pharaohs' signet ring. That meant he had the authority of the Pharaoh behind him. He could make decrees and rule. Also, he was given robes of fine linen to wear, and the Pharaoh put an expensive gold chain around his neck. He was given a chariot to ride in and wherever he went royal guards cried out before him, "Bow down!" He was given a palace to live in, with many servants and a wife was chosen for him. You can bet she was probably the most beautiful woman they could find for him. In one single day Joseph went from prison to a new life that was totally amazing. Joseph's faithfulness paid off! Promotion came!

What about you? Would you like to be promoted? You can go as far and as high in the kingdom of God as you want to go. That is the way God made it. You can be as close to God as you want to be. Start moving closer to Him. Start passing your tests. The more you pass the higher you can go. If you think Joseph's promotion was exciting, wait till you see how God promotes His own! Don't think like I thought, that is fine for Joseph, but I am a nobody.

You are Important to God

If you are like I was, you feel insignificant and you think God has more important things to do than pay attention to you. In fact, I thought I had to make a lot of noise and do a lot of complaining so that He would remember that I existed. I wanted Him to see the messes I was always in and get to work. I thought He must be forgetting about me, so I would do a lot of belly aching to Him, to remind Him of just how hard things were for me.

That is how I felt for a long time. But I have since learned that I was wrong. I now know that He is intimately involved in my life. It is just not on His agenda to make my life the piece of cake I want to be. He is testing me so He can promote me. In fact, I have come to realize that The Father, Jesus and the Holy Spirit get together and have staff meetings to discuss just what is best for me, just like They do for you.

God is forming character in us. He has eternal positions He is preparing us for, positions of honor. Like Joseph we are not on an easy path. We are called to greatness. We are called to follow Christ, to become joint heirs with Him in His kingdom. But I also have a part to play in all this, a big part, doing what I am supposed to do. Getting busy and passing my tests. Then I can move on.

The Book of Proverbs is a Good Study Manual

I love the book of Proverbs. My son and I studied the book of Proverbs together when he was a preteen. It is a good study manual for passing the tests of life. It warns of the pitfalls out in the world and the tests that are coming and tells you how to pass. Chapter one tells us the fear of the Lord is the beginning of wisdom. In other words, we need to please God! {Joseph's secret} Then we learn to obey our parents. There is more good stuff coming. We learn that sinners are going to try to entice us to join them, they are out for ill-gotten gain, but they actually way lay themselves and it ruins their own life. Young men are warned of the sexual immorality awaiting them. The seductress is described, and we see the fool being waylaid by her, but we find her house leads to death. Oh, and there is more, we learn how to handle money. How to succeed in everything we do. Who to spend time with, who not to spend time with. How to be blessed and what will ruin us. It warns of strong drink and sudden riches. It tells us to work hard and warns against laziness. The book of Proverbs tells us how important the words we speak are, and the importance of honesty.

Everything we need to know to pass the tests of life is written in the book of Proverbs. I wish the book of Proverbs was studied in every High School, young people would know what is coming and how to face it. If young people studied the book of Proverbs, we would put Dr. Phil out of business. All of life's pitfalls and how to avoid them were written about thousands of years ago and they are more relevant today than ever.

What Else?

I think there is more to passing tests. They are enlarging us on the inside. They are forming us into the image of Christ. Our tests are maturing us, preparing us and changing us. They are increasing our capacity to love, to forgive, for joy, and for peace. They are making us mature in Christ. They are increasing our faith.

We see Joseph advance from a spoiled seventeen-year-old boy whose bragging caused his brothers to hate him, to a mature man who changed the then known world and saved his father's family. A man with great authority that did not abuse it. But his tests were sure extreme.

Maybe we need to change the way we look at trials, or tests. The book of James tells us, *My brethren count it all joy when you fall into various trials, knowing that the testing of your faith produces patience. But let patience have its perfect work, that you may be perfect and complete lacking nothing. James 1:2-3* Do we want to be perfect and complete lacking nothing? Then we need tests.

The Purpose of Tests

So remember, God knows right where you are, He sees you. Remember the life of Joseph and be faithful to

God. He will promote you in due time. Choosing to do right will never go unnoticed by God. Choosing to do right consistently, no matter what, like Joseph did, it will lead to blessings, blessings and more blessings. It will lead to maturity and increase your faith; it will enlarge you on the inside, increase your position and form you into the image of Christ! Tests are developing your patience and causing you to be perfect and complete, lacking nothing. The purposes for tests in your life are for your own good, to bring about growth and promotion.

Chapter Five

Light and Darkness

For God did not send His Son into the world to condemn the world, but that the world through Him might be saved. He who believes in Him is not condemned; but he who does not believe is condemned already; because he has not believed in the name of the only begotten Son of God. And this is the condemnation, that light has come into the world, and men loved darkness rather than the light, because their deeds were evil. For everyone practicing evil hates the light and does not come to the light, lest his deeds be exposed. But he who does the truth comes to the light, that his deeds may be clearly seen, that they have been done in God. John 3:17-21

To pass the test of life we need to come to the light.

What is Light?

Light is amazing stuff. There are many definitions of light. One is **light: the form of energy that makes it possible to see things.** Another definition is **truth.**

We know some things about light. Light is a form of energy. Light moves at 186,281 miles per second. {That is pretty fast} There is light that is not visible to the human eye, in fact only a small portion is visible to the human eye. Light is part of the electromagnetic spectrum which ranges from radio waves to gamma waves. Visible light is right in the middle of seven electromagnetic waves. It goes from radio waves to microwaves, infrared to visible light then ultraviolet, x-rays and finally gamma rays. How interesting that there are seven, God often does things in sevens.

Also, there is a connection of light to color. Without light there is no color. The rainbow comes from light and there are seven colors in the rainbow. They are red, orange, yellow, green, blue indigo and violet. Here is another seven.

There is another thing God did in a seven; He created the earth in seven days. And it was the first day that God created light. Genesis 1:3 *Then God said, "Let there be light'; and there was light.* This light is not to be confused with the sun which God did not create until day four. God created some other kind of light on day one, energy. A light that is not visible to us, in our present state. Although it is very possible that in the garden before the fall that more light was visible to Adam. We know Adam walked in a higher plane than we do now. He could walk and talk with God. He could communicate with animals. He could also eat of trees that had spiritual fruit. And how come he didn't know he was naked? Was he clothed with light?

We get into some deep science when we talk about light, the kind that causes me to scratch my head. Like Einstein's theory of E= Mc, I have no idea what that is all about even though I read a whole book on it one time. I think it has to do with matter and energy being interchangeable. This is deep science and I want to get back to spiritual things except for one point I want to make first. Science is spiritual. When we start talking about light and energy and matter and the things of the spirit we are talking about the same things. The Bible is a book of science, and God is the creator and everything He has created is the subject of science. Quantum physics will only lead you to God; in fact, all true science will only lead you to God.

God, Jesus and Us

Let's get back to light and darkness and passing the tests of life. Jesus told us in, John *8:12* that **He is the light of the world.** Jesus is our light. We also are told in1John 1:5 that **God is light and in Him there is no darkness at all**. God our Father is light; that is very interesting. God is the source of light. It doesn't say that He has light but that He is light.

We also know when we become saved God puts His light in us. Matthew 5:14 Jesus tells us, "**You are the light of the world.**"

We don't realize how literal this is because we don't see this light with our physical eyes. It is not visible. But it is there, and it is visible in another realm. We know that there are things we cannot see and hear and yet they are present. They are at a frequency that is undetectable to humans. We know when we blow a dog whistle, that we cannot hear anything, but a dog hears it. They can hear that frequency. Just the same there are many things around us we do not see or perceive, because they operate at a different frequency, they are spiritual.

Summer Feels the Light

I have learned to discern when angels come to my house from heaven. Heaven is very bright and the angels that come to earth from heaven especially straight from God's throne, the center of brightness, are extremely bright. They are so bright that even though I can't see the brightness I can feel it. The first time I felt it was an incident I wrote about in my book, *Satan Has No Power Over You*. I was having trouble with demonic activity during the night. This particular day I was reading a book that spoke of a deliverance angel. I had not known there was such an angel. I put the book down and hollered, "God, You have a delivering angel, I want him, send him to me!!"

All the rest of that day I told my children an angel was going to come that night. That night the angel did come, I awoke and felt a presence of light on the side of my bed. I could also feel the darkness on the other side, but it left. Because the brightness coming from this angel was so powerful. I could not see it, but I sure could feel it.

Not only did I feel the brightness I felt a strong vibration, and when the angel touched me, I felt like a million volts of electricity went through me. It was light, pure light. I have had this happen many times since then and when it does, I know there is an angel from heaven in the room. I can tell right where the angel is standing because I can feel the brightness and there is a vibration and power that I will feel.

A couple of years ago a friend of mine named Laurie was sick. Laurie was in her late eighties, and she was the most amazing woman I had ever met. She loved people to a degree that I could hardly even understand. But not only that, she was also so happy. She was always happy. I used to come twice a week to give her a bath. I would go into her bedroom and wake her up for her bath and she would amaze me. I would shake her a little and then she would open her eyes. Immediately she would smile a huge smile and yell, {She was hard of hearing], "My Summer!!" Then she would close her eyes in glee and say, "It's a beeeeeautiful day!"

I could not imagine waking up happy. I hate waking up. I asked her husband one day, "Does she wake up like that every day?"

"Every day," he told me.

Laurie also had no concept of time. She was so happy in the moment, and she enjoyed each moment so much that she would relish it. She never ever got anywhere on time because she was always so happy where she was and who she was with, and she was slow to leave because of it. It was hard for me to get her shower done in two hours even though I did most people's showers in one, because she was relishing every minute of her shower.

I enjoyed about eight wonderful years seeing Laurie twice a week. She would always tell me I was her Summer. My family only borrowed me because I belonged to her.

Laurie was ill and her family had gathered around. The only ones not present were her beloved sister Mary and her daughter Susan, who lived in Florida and couldn't get there. When I came into Laurie's house that day, I tried to wake her for a bed bath, she opened her eyes for a second and did her huge smile for just a second but then she faded back to a semi coma.

I thought, as I left that day, that death could still be a couple weeks away. I had been with many dying patients and many times it goes on for days or even weeks. I was wrong. That night I woke up and I could feel that powerful light in my room, the vibration and the energy and the familiar feeling. It was standing right next to my bed. I knew there was an angel from heaven standing by my bed, but I wondered why. He stood there a few minutes and then he was gone.

Suddenly I knew. Laurie had passed away. I looked at my clock to note the time. It was 3:20 am. I had to laugh because I knew that angel had come to take Laurie to heaven, but she wouldn't go right away. I knew she would insist to first go see Mary, her beloved sister. Then she would see Susan, her daughter, and then she must have insisted on coming to see me.

I knew exactly what that angel was going through trying to get Laurie moving because I had done it for eight years. She just wanted to visit and relish one last time with her loved ones, and she was in no hurry to get to heaven. Also, I felt honored she stopped to see me before heaven. She had never been to my house before. The next morning her husband called me to tell me she had passed away about 3:05 am.

This light has become very real to me even though I cannot see it. I can feel it and it is a very powerful feeling. I felt God in this way, one time, and it felt like the angels from heaven do only times one million. My body literally convulsed in His presence from the power of His light. I thought I was going to die; I was literally undone. {I still loved it though}

Darkness

The opposite of light is darkness. Darkness is not amazing like light is. It is the absence of light. There is no color in darkness, it is just darkness. Darkness can be defined as **the total lack of light** it is also defined as **evil.** I also know the feeling of darkness. I lived every day in deep darkness before I got saved. I was a miserable human being. I think that is why I love light so much. It felt so good to come out of the darkness that I never want to be there again.

Two Kingdoms

There are two kingdoms that exist in the spirit

realm; they are the Kingdom of Light and the kingdom of darkness. We automatically are born into the kingdom of darkness because of the fall of Adam. To pass the test of life we have to change kingdoms to the Kingdom of Light and become children of the light. Jesus delivers us from darkness when we turn our lives to Him. *Colossians 1:13* says *Who hath delivered us from the power of darkness and hath translated us into the kingdom of His dear Son.*

We are to come into the light. We are to change kingdoms. We are to walk in His light. We read about walking in the light in Ephesians 5:8-11 *For you were once darkness, but now you are light in the Lord. Walk as children of the light {for the fruit of the Spirit is in all goodness righteousness and truth} finding out what is acceptable to the Lord. And have no fellowship with the unfruitful works of darkness, but rather expose them.* We see in this verse it is up to us to begin to walk in light and to disassociate ourselves with the works of darkness.

Now that we have changed kingdoms, we emit a light, although this light is not visible to the human realm it is still there and very real just like visible light. Actually, every human being emits a light, but some emit a dark light.

Jesus spoke of this in *Matthew 6:22-23 "The lamp of the body is the eye. If therefore your eye is good your whole body will be full of light. But if your eye is bad, your whole body will be full of darkness. If the light that is in you is darkness, how great is that darkness!"*

We see light and good go together and darkness and evil. They are two opposite poles like two magnets that attract opposite things. We also see that we emit either light or dark light depending on how we are living. When we emit light, we attract good. We attract blessings. Also, we attract angelic activity because they can see us, and they are attracted to the light.

The same is true with darkness, when we emit darkness, we attract curses, we also attract demonic activity and although everyone has angels it is difficult for them to see in the darkness that surrounds you.

My sister, daughter and I found this out not too long ago at our prayer meeting. We were praying for the children in our families when one of their angels asked us to please teach them some scripture so they could see them better. Just a couple scriptures would help they said. I don't want my grandchildren in the dark, let's speak scripture over our children and teach them scripture! Let's keep them in the light.

What Affects Our Light?

Just because we are Christians doesn't automatically exempt us from darkness. Our thoughts have an effect on darkness or light. Negative thoughts produce darkness. Depression, fear or unforgiveness or hatred, these things emit a darkness that attracts demons to you and causes your life to produce negative things.

Walking in the light means dealing with these things the way Jesus told us to, such as forgive your brother seventy times seven and loving your enemies. Love and forgiveness produce light. Positive thoughts produce light. We are told in *Philippians 4:8, Finally brethren, whatever things are just whatever things are pure whatever things are lovely, whatever things are of good report, if there is any virtue and if there is anything praiseworthy—meditate on these things.*

But that's not all; our words attract either darkness or light. The words on television and movies these days are so foul and filthy and full of darkness, and they keep getting darker. In fact, our country has become in gross darkness. We have to come out of the gross darkness and evil deeds and walk in the light. We also have to speak as children of the light. *Proverbs 18:21* tells us, *Death and life are in the power of the tongue.*

Speaking truth of course is light but lying attracts darkness. There are no little white lies! They are black, black, black! So, lying and cursing and foul course language is out. We want to speak positive and uplifting and praise to God. And we always want to give a good report.

There are places of darkness. Places we do not need to be in unless we are sent by God to minister to someone. These are bars of course and casinos and fortune tellers and places where evil is done. They are full of evil spirits and darkness. There is music which attracts darkness and music which attracts light. I just instinctively threw away my record collection the day after I got saved; the darkness in them that used to attract me now repelled me. I began to listen to Christian music because its ministered light to me. {Not that anything not Christian is bad, there is a lot of good music that doesn't attract darkness.}

There are even smells that attract darkness and smells that attract light. Some incenses and of course the smell of marijuana attract darkness. Those who have visited heaven or hell always comment on the smells. Hell of course has hideous smell of rotting flesh. And I have heard in heaven many tell of smelling a citrus smell, that is lovely and of course the smells of flowers.

There are other things as well that radiate darkness. One extremely dark thing is pornography. Districts where much illicit sex items and prostitution and dirty bookstores are, they are very dark, and you don't have to be really spiritual to feel it. Even clothes can attract light or darkness. Some are subtle, once I had to throw away a pair of earrings, I thought were cute. They were a little pair of pink dice. But I felt something weird about them.

Some clothes are not so subtle, I have seen some kids whose clothes and make up cause them to look like vampires. Of course, they attract darkness. Many clothes have skulls or peace signs on them. And clothes should be modest and cover us appropriately.

We have two completely opposite kingdoms operating on earth. They operate in two polar opposites. One is good and one is bad. One is light and one is darkness. One is from God, and one is from the devil. One leads to heaven, and one leads to hell. To pass the test of life we need to come out of the one and come into the other. We need to leave darkness and walk in light. It is a real light. The closer we get to God the brighter we will be.

It also means becoming a light to the world. As we walk down our own road, we want to become brighter and brighter as we grow closer to the source of light, Jesus, He is the Light of the world.

Chapter Six

The Love Test

*Though I speak with the tongues of men and angels, but
have not love, I have become a sounding brass or a
clanging symbol. And though I have the gift of prophecy,
and understand all mysteries and all knowledge, and
though I have all faith, so that I could remove mountains,
but have not love, I am nothing. And though I bestow all
my goods to feed the poor, and though I give my body to
be burned, but have not love, it profits me nothing.*
1 Corinthians 13:1-3

Did You Learn to Love?

The prophet and wonderful man of God, Bob
Jones, had a heavenly experience when he nearly died. On
August 8, 1975, an aneurism erupted in Bob's abdomen,
and it seemed that Bob died. During this experience Bob
saw and learned many things. One of the things he learned
was the importance of learning to love in this life.

Bob found himself standing before the Lord. He

was standing in a line waiting to see the Lord. Next to Bob was a faceless man he said was the Holy Spirit. There were several others before him in line.

The first one, in this line, was a black woman who was surrounded by many angels. Bob wondered why she had so many angels standing with her. The faceless man explained to Bob that she had been a mighty minister on the earth and these angels had helped her. As this woman stood before the Lord, the Lord asked her, "Did you learn to love?"

The woman answered, "Yes."

And the Lord reached out and kissed her and then He drew her into Himself. Bob saw she went into heaven through the Lord Jesus. He was like a door, and she and all the angels with her went in, through Jesus. She had learned to love.

The second person in the line was an eleven-year-old girl who had just died. She had been confined to bed during her life because of illness. Instead of becoming bitter she had spent her time praying for others. When she stood before Jesus, He asked her, "Did you learn to love?" She also replied, "Yes." And then she entered heaven through the Lord.

The next one in line before Bob was a very elderly woman. When the Lord asked her if she had learned to love, her reply was different. In that place, only the truth was told. She replied to the Lord, "I only loved you, Lord. I became bitter and did not love others."

She was saved and entered in just as the others, but she had no works that could be rewarded as the others did. She did not pass the love test.

Jesus commanded us to love in *John 15:12 This is my commandment that you love one another as I have loved you.* In fact, when Jesus was asked *in Matthew 22: 36*, what was the greatest commandment He replied, *"You shall love the Lord your God with all your heart, with all your soul and with all your mind. This is the first and greatest commandment. And the second is like it: You shall love your neighbor as yourself. On these two commandments hang all the Law and the Prophets* .We are given a test to pass in our lifetime, a test of eternal importance. It is the test of learning to love. One of the most important tests you will ever take in this lifetime does not require intellectual intelligence. In fact, this eleven-year-old girl passed this test very young. There are those who have passed this test that are mentally retarded. There are those who have passed this test that have nothing. To pass this test only requires using the love God has placed inside you and giving it your all.

This older woman, who only halfway passed the love test, had allowed herself to get bitter. In order to pass the love, test we cannot allow ourselves to get bitter. We have to forgive. We have to be determined to obey this commandment of God's.

There are those who pass this test against incredible odds. Those who have never known love, themselves. Those who were abused as a child and never experienced the love most of us receive from our families. Those who have faced physical, mental and sexual abuse, from the time they can remember, and are filled with rage.

And yet, they muster every bit of love they have and refuse to pass on the abuse.

Passing Against all Odds

That is my husband Jim's story. I wrote more about it in my first book, *The Impossible Marriage*. God surprised me when He told me my husband Jim had a much higher place in heaven than I did, and that Jim was much more pleasing to Him than I was. I was astounded.

My husband was a Christian and was trying to serve the Lord, but I didn't think he was doing so well. He seemed like a real sinner to me. He was an alcoholic and grew up in trouble, always he was in trouble. He began committing felonies as a preteen. And now he had a lot of difficulty staying out of trouble as an adult and he was filled with rage. And yet, this uneducated man who had spent his childhood and part of his adult life locked up in institutions, used his all.

He has always brought home his paycheck he has earned to support us, his wife and three children. He used as little as possible to support his addictions. He never passed on the abuse he experienced to his children, in fact, he told our children every single day that he loved them and still does even though they are adults.

My husband did not know how to love because he did not know what love was, but he used what he had. My husband knows how to cook. That is how my husband Jim shows love, with food.

I was in high school when we were going together,

and Jim fed me. Every day between school and work Jim had a meal waiting for me. He could make anything taste good. He would make spinach and eggs on pumpernickel bread, or bacon sandwiches with a side of great northern beans. He just lived in a rented room, but he would get permission to use the kitchen and make me something to eat.

When we got married, and had our own kitchen, I worked the afternoon shift and after work every night was a feast. Chicken strips and French fries or a hamburger topped with tomato and lettuce and shakes from the blender. Jim was showing me love the only way he knew how.

When our three kids came along Jim loved them with food. I never bought a jar of baby food. Jim kept the highchair next to him and he would feed the baby off his plate. He would cook and then chop up the food in tiny pieces and feed them. Through all three kids, the highchair was always next to his chair. And when he came home from work his pockets had candy in them for little children to find.

His day off meant dinner, fried chicken and corn with whipped mashed potatoes and butter. And he always sat down last. He would serve us like a waiter and make sure we all had enough and then he sat down with us.

One day, that especially stands out in my mind; Jim had stayed home from church. When we got home, like usual, a feast was prepared but the funny thing was, Jim was on roller skates. We lived in a horrible old one room apartment with no carpeting and while we ate, he skated around us serving us a dinner fit for kings. He rolled up to the table serving us helpings and twirled around on his way back to the kitchen, doing a few spins and rolled back to fill our drinks. That was how he loved us.

Yes, there were many sleepless nights when Jim was drunk, he would pound on the walls and scream for hours, he was tormented by his past, our life was not easy. But we knew Jim loved us, he loved us with breakfasts in bed and picnics, and not just us but others too. Jim would bring food to the neighbors and cook for anyone that came over, a repairman, or anyone that stopped by. I have seen him give a homeless man staying with a neighbor the last of the food in our fridge. That is how he loves. Yes, Jim has learned how to love.

Yes, there are those who pass the love test, even though they look like failures to others and have never received love. They pass because they use the love they have. There is something amazing that happens when you use the love you have. When you muster up everything inside you, when your filled with rage or when you want to hate, when you want to return evil for evil, when you want to get even, or when you don't want to share, but you do share, or you do one of the many other ways to show love. When you feel like you can't love, but you do. A miracle happens. That love inside you grows, it multiplies.

God is a magnificent multiplier and when you give Him what you have, He gives you more. And something else is happening too. You begin to look a little more like your creator.

God is Love. There is joy in love. There is every

good thing in love. No one ever becomes happy by being selfish or cruel and unkind. Unforgiveness and jealousy and bitterness will never give us a minute of happiness. Love rewards those who live by it. The rewards are eternal. It creates a never-ending circle of goodness which only gets bigger. Love, true love, God's kind of love, even loves its enemies. The more love we have inside of us is the more of God we have. What will you say, when God asks you, "Did you learn to love?"

I hope you will say, "Yes."

Chapter Seven

Get Out of the Second Heaven!

I have been failing some of the same tests all of my life. I just can't seem to pass them. I know what I have to do. I struggle and struggle and sometimes I make a little progress and I think I have made it. But the test comes again, and I am back to square one. These tests have to do with fear. There are some things that happen that scare me, the same situations over and over, and every time they happen again, I panic. I have several of these areas in my life but the worse one has to do with my husband's drinking.

It all goes back to my very early childhood when I was still in my crib. I had a stepfather who was not only a pedophile he was sadistic. All my uncontrollable fears in life seem to stem from him. I have been afraid of men, going to bed at night, animals, but the worst one of all is smelling alcohol on some one's breath. It is not a normal fear. It is a choking, paralyzing fear. It takes over, and I cannot function. I feel absolute terror and I want to hide!

I married an alcoholic. I wrote the whole story in

my book, *The Impossible Marriage.* I married an alcoholic, with huge rejection issues. I am writing this book several years after writing, *The Impossible Marriage.* I still have struggles with this same test, and my husband still has drinking slips!

One of my biggest issues with God about writing that book was I thought we were still too big of a mess! {Especially me} I really struggled. It took more than a year after God told me to write it before I wrote a single word.

Then I assumed that God would fix things, and Jim would never ever slip again, now that the book was published. And for a while it seemed like that might be true, things seemed peaceful in our lives. Jim wasn't drinking, and I wasn't cowering in fear praying to die.

But even if Jim was sober, I still had some fear. If he didn't come home on time I wondered. Was he drinking? Why is he sucking on that candy? Is he trying to hide alcohol on his breath?

I only saw two solutions to this problem. One is for God to totally deliver my husband, so he never ever drinks again. The other is for me to die and go to Heaven. I am tired of this torment.

Really the only thing as bad as things used to be is my fear. Things have really improved but they used to be unbearable. My husband, when he would drink would go into rages that would last for hours. I had three kids to worry about and nowhere to go to get away from him. Now, my husband rarely drinks but when he does there is no temper, and my kids are grown. And my daughter Joy lives a mile and a half down the road; I can escape and cry, and beg God to take me home to Him, at her house. But Jim still feels rejected when I leave. In fact, that is why he drinks to overcome his feelings of rejection.

One day, about two years ago it happened again. I came home from work to a drunk husband. FEAR!!! I grabbed his keys and mine and took off to Joy's house. I pulled into her driveway and God said, "Go home!"

So, I went home. I halfway passed the test. I went home and of course Jim wanted me near him. I totally understand why my husband drinks. He is so tormented by his past and the abuse and rejection he faced in his early years. It makes my past seem like nothing. And then when he does drink, he is so mad at himself that he needs some acceptance.

I knew it, but I couldn't do it. The fear, like a giant stood between me and Jim and I couldn't get to him. Somewhere inside me I wanted to hold him and comfort him. But I couldn't get past the giant of fear. So, I went home and with gritted teeth I told him, "I will stay home but you stay in our bedroom, and I will stay in the upstairs bedroom but stay away from me!"

"Do you forgive me?" he slurred.

"Yes!" I hissed and marched upstairs and cried myself to sleep.

Somehow, inside me, I know this test will not go away until I pass it. I keep telling myself I will do better and sometimes I do, but with gritted teeth, I really want to run and hide.

One day, not long ago, after another round of this, I marched around the next day still reeling from all the emotions I had been through, so I went down to my daughter Joy's house for prayer.

As she began to pray for me, she immediately heard from the Lord. She opened her eyes and said to me, "Mom you need to stay out of the second heaven. The second heaven is where Satan operates. Every time dad drinks you get in the emotional realm and respond in fear. I saw a picture of you while we were praying you look like a little kid who is running away from home, you know…., they have a little stick with their stuffed tied up in a handkerchief."

"You mean a hobo stick?" I asked.

"Yes," Joy continued, "the hobo stick you are carrying around is all the things that make you afraid. And when they happen you respond to them in fear, and you want to run away. You act in fear and in fear there is torment."

When she used the word torment, she hit the nail on the head. Torment is the word I would use to describe how I feel many times. And she hit the nail on the head about the fears I carry. I know exactly what they are. Alcohol is the biggest one, but I also have a fear of losing my job and losing everything. Therefore, any minor problem at work also sends me into a tailspin. Although, through the years my bundle of fears has gotten smaller these two big ones I was still carrying. I couldn't believe someone was finally understanding exactly how I feel and describing it to me. Is it any wonder I constantly tell God to take me to heaven? I live in torment.

I was hanging on to every word that she said

because I so wanted to live without this fear and torment.

"Perfect love casts out fear," Joy continued, "when something happens, you are to go straight to the throne of God before you respond, and He will tell you how to respond. No more stopping in the second heaven, you go straight to throne of God."

I felt such hope, that maybe I could finally get past this torment I have lived with as long as I can remember.

"Let's go to throne right now," Joy said. "There is an angel here to put you in a bubble and bring you straight to the throne."

She sent me straight to throne of God. I couldn't see any bubble, but I tried to picture one. I felt such peace and acceptance that I thought I will just pop in here next time something happens and get this peace and God will tell me what to do. Then I won't have to live in fear anymore. It hasn't been quite that easy, it is a process.

If Satan can keep us trapped in that emotional realm, he can keep us running away in fear when our big issues come up. We deal with God on a spiritual level, and we defeat Satan on a spiritual level because when we move to the spiritual arena we are above the devil in a place where Jesus has already defeated him. We are seated in heavenly places in our spirit man. We are in Christ.

Well, I have to confess something to you. The next time my husband drank came the next day. {my test} I tried to go straight to the throne room but all I felt was still, that choking fear. I tried not to do my usual falling apart, but it still felt the same. I tried to get quiet and pray and go straight to the throne of God, but lately I have been so spiritually blind I couldn't seem to find God at all. But I tried. I had been going through a long dry spell spiritually. The only time I can hear God is when I am writing books, {He helps me write.} So, I called a friend to help me pray and went to bed.

The next day as soon as I got some time alone, I got quiet and tried to hear God. I didn't give up even though I couldn't. I was determined. After some time, my phone rang, it was my daughter, Joy. I was surprised to hear from her because she works three twelve-hour shifts on the weekends, and she is usually either at work or sleeping. But I sensed God was answering my determination with some help from Joy. She encouraged me again.

Joy had such peace and faith, she sent me to heaven in a bubble again and I no longer felt afraid, I felt peace. I love peace. I was so glad I had my daughter to help me.

A couple of days later Joy called me, and she was hysterical. Where was this calm voice of reason? Every time Joy called me upset it was about the same thing. She had a certain situation that sent her into a tailspin, every single time. I stopped her ranting, and told her," Let's pray."

As I prayed with her, I realized she needed the same advice she had given me. She needed to stay out of the second heaven; she needed to go directly to throne of God. She was trapped in the emotional arena and Satan was putting her through the wringer emotionally. This certain situation, which she was upset about, again, was her trigger. It wasn't so much fear, with Joy, as anger.

"Joy," I said, "You need to go straight to the second heaven like you told me."

Joy was silent for a second as my words sunk in; I thought I had gotten through to her. Then she said, "But, mom, this is a real problem, not like you and dad." Then she hung up.   Suddenly I realized something, Joy had the same problem I did, it just looked a little different. Especially to Joy, my problems looked easy to her and hers looked hard. She was having a constant battle that would pull her from her place of victory. I missed the Joy who had called me the day before, in faith and undefeatable.

Then I realized something else too. My best friend Rhonda, every time she would call upset, it was for the same reason, her health. We had been praying for the same thing for years. Her health triggered a fear in her of dying, because she was raising four boys alone and she didn't want to die and leave them alone. It was a battle she could not win because she was fighting it in the second heaven. She was constantly defeated, in this area, like I was in mine. She had health problems regularly.

I thought of my sister, she had another issue that sent her reeling, a daughter who was always in trouble. Every time my sister got in peace, some new disaster with her daughter would knock her flat.

I suddenly saw Satan's strategy in all our lives was to keep us in a realm where he could win the battle. That realm is the soul, the mind, will and emotions. If Satan can get us to fight him there, he will win every time.

There is a realm where Satan stands defeated

already, defeated by the blood of Jesus and that is the realm of the Spirit, the Holy Spirit. It is not as hard as it sounds because God has placed His kingdom, His Holy Spirit right inside of you. We have access to the throne of God. We can go directly to God; to a place Satan is already defeated.

When we are there, out of Satan's reach, we know it, because, the place is peace, and the place is joy and the place is rest, and the place is trust in God and the place is faith. When we are there, this is very dangerous for the devil. He can't hurt you! He has to get you back down to his arena. So, he pulls on our triggers. Mine is my husband's drinking.

So, what happened to me when I learned this? I got in peace and Jim never drank again, right?

Not exactly. Actually, what really happened was Jim had a total meltdown. He lost control of his drinking totally. He hadn't been taking his medicine properly and I hadn't even noticed, {I am supposed to be supervising his meds}. His mental health also went into a tailspin. He was acting crazy. I had to take away his car keys and credit card because he lost all control. I would come home from work, and he was still drunk. He got into trouble with the law again also.

Jim could not even get any help. He tried to get admitted to the drug and alcohol rehab at the hospital, but they would not take him because his mental illness was out of control. They told him to admit himself to the psychiatric ward of the hospital. So, he called them, but they wouldn't take him because his alcohol use was out of control. They wanted him to go to the rehab first.

Everything in my life was totally amuck! I had so much fear I could hardly breathe. How am I supposed to function? Am I even going to be able to keep our house? Is my life over?

Yes. In a sense my life was over.

It got so severe I told God, "My life is over, if you want this mess, take it, take all of it."

Something happened to me. I thought about God, and how I have been through this stuff before. He can handle my life. I can't figure this thing out. In the midst of my storm, I left the soul realm, and I went straight to the lap of my Father.

The fear left.

There was about a month or more Jim kept drinking. I put my arms around my husband daily, alcohol and all. I told him, "Whatever happens, I love you. I will never leave you." I meant it. No more gritted teeth.

Jim kept trying and finally got admitted to a rehab facility. He has been sober more than four months now. He has finally got his medicine straightened out, also.

Somehow, in the middle of the worst of this situation, I managed to stay out of the second heaven.

Is it possible to have peace in the midst of a storm? Is it possible to see your whole life fall apart and to wonder what will become of you and not be afraid? Is it possible to see your loved ones in danger and you don't even know how to help them and to still have hope? Is it possible to face the same test over and over, for your whole life and finally pass it?

There is a place above your problems, a place where Satan can't hurt you, a place of victory, and a safe place. That place is our home.

Yes, it is possible to have peace in the midst of a storm. I think I passed my test this time.

{Authors note, I actually started this chapter over six months ago, I couldn't finish it. All this stuff happened between the time I began this chapter and ended this chapter. When you write books, you get tested}

Chapter Eight

The Marriage Test

Drink water from your own cistern And running water from your own well. Should your fountains be dispersed abroad, Streams of water in the streets? Let them be your own, and not for strangers with you. Let your fountain be blessed and rejoice with the wife of your youth. As a loving deer and a graceful doe, let her breasts satisfy you at all times; And always be enraptured by her love. For why should you my son, be enraptured by an immoral woman, and embraced by the arms of a seductress? Proverbs 5:15-20

Everything God does is so amazing and awesome and wonderful and holy. Marriage is one of those things. Marriage, the way God made it, is beautiful and fulfilling and holy. And like everything else that comes from God it is good and it is meant to bring joy and blessing.

The mate God gives you is the ultimate blessing from God, prepared just for you, meant for your good for your growth and for your blessing. Your mate is also a huge responsibility and a huge test. Marriage is a huge way you can show your faithfulness to God. That person lying in bed next to you, {And you better be married to them if they are in bed next to you} is a tangible, piece of God in your life. They were brought to you by God, and how you treat them is one of the most important tests in your life. Don't take it lightly.

The Prototype for Marriage

Let's look at the first marriage God created Adam and Eve. *And the Lord God said, "It is not good that man should be alone; I will make him a helper comparable to him." Genesis 2:18   And the Lord God caused a deep sleep to fall on Adam, and he slept; and He took one of his ribs and closed up the flesh in its place. Then the rib which the Lord God had taken from the man He made into a woman, and He brought her to the man. And Adam said: "This is now bone of my bones and flesh of my flesh; She will be called Woman, because she was taken out of Man." Therefore, a man shall leave his father and mother and be joined to his wife, and they shall become one flesh. And they were both naked, the man and his wife, and were not ashamed. Genesis 2:21-25*

God, in His very great love, is amazingly good to Adam. He has made this beautiful world for Adam to live in, which was perfect at the time. The fall of man had caused the imperfections on earth, such as storms, poisonous insects or animals even thorn and thistles. The earth as Adam knew it was a paradise. Adam is in authority over the earth. God has put Adam over the animals which Adam lovingly chooses names for, and Adam is in charge here.

Adam is also a gardener. He lives in a beautiful garden which God has planted for Him. And God walks with Adam on the earth and has fellowship with Him. God is very good to Adam but now God brings Adam the ultimate gift. God is about to institute marriage.

He forms Eve, from Adams own body. He forms Eve from Adam's rib. Now God presents Eve to Adam. It is hard to imagine Adam's delight as God brings Adam this beautiful creature, a true match for him. Not only was she beautiful, but this woman God also presented to him, she was naked. To say Adam was delighted is an understatement. It was God's plan now that they produce a family.

Adam and Eve belong to one another; they are truly a gift of God to each other. Now Adam has a new type of garden. He has seed which he plants in the womb of his wife which produces children. Together they co create, with God, children.

Adam and Eve receive the huge responsibility and privilege of bringing new lives into the world. What could be more precious and holy? God has entrusted the man and woman with a huge responsibility. Here is the prototype of marriage, one man and one woman coming together and cleaving to one another and becoming one flesh and establishing a family. This family is God's design, and it is holy. Following this design causes blessings on you and your children and their children. It is a fountain of blessing. A loving godly marriage multiplies and grows a healthy family and healthy generations after you. It is no wonder Satan so attacks the family.

Valuing Marriage

My purpose for this chapter is to reawaken us to the awesome gift and responsibility of marriage to respect it and treat it as the holy thing that God has created it to be. And to unmask the deceptions in today's world; to show the true ugliness and destructiveness of adultery and fornication. So that just the mere thought of adultery becomes repulsive, vile and a trampling of what is good and holy. Do you think I am being over dramatic? Well let me read you a few things the Bible has to say about sex sin.

To keep you from the evil woman, From the flattering tongue of a seductress. Do not lust after her beauty in your heart, nor let her allure you with her eyelids. For by means of a harlot a man is reduced to a crust of bread; and an adulteress will prey on his precious life. Can a man take fire into his bosom, And his clothes not be burned? Can one walk on hot coals And his feet not be seared? So is he who goes into his neighbor's wife; Whoever touches her will not be innocent. Proverbs 6:24-29

In the next chapter we read, *Do not stray into her paths; For she has cast down many wounded, And all who were slain by her were strong men. Her house is the way to hell, Descending to the chambers of death. Proverbs 7: 25- 27*

These verses are talking about adultery and are just as relevant for a woman as for a man. There are people who wouldn't dream of using someone else's toothbrush but will commit adultery or fornication! Which is worse?

Sex sin involves contaminating not just the physical body but the soul realm and the spirit realm also. God has designed sex for marriage and only for marriage and there are some things that take place only meant for the married couple. Let's talk about all three ways this sin does harm.

The Physical Realm

Do you not know that your bodies are members of Christ Himself? Shall I then take the members of Christ and unite them with a prostitute? Never! Do you not know that he who unites *himself with a prostitute is one with her in body? For it is said, "The two will become one flesh." But he who unites himself with the Lord is one with Him in spirit. **Flee from sexual immorality.** All other sins a man commits are outside his body **but he who sins sexually sins against his own body.*** 1 Corinthians 6:15-18

In our times sex sin is rampant. In fact, it has become the normal. But we have to be different! Passing the tests of life means doing things God's way, not the world's way. That is why I want to expose the world's way for what it is, WRONG!!!

First, we will talk about the body. There are many diseases that can be passed through sex. Some, once contacted, will be in your body for the rest of your life. Even those people, who occasionally have illicit sex, with someone they are dating, are opening themselves up to a lot of bad junk. Think of sex as a stream. Proverbs said it like this drinking water from your own well. Those who are married and faithful have a pure stream. For those who are practicing illicit sex, it is a sewer.

Let say we have a young woman will call her Sarah. She dates a young man named Bill. He talks Sarah into sex before marriage. She loves him, so she goes ahead. Well, Bill has had three other relationships before Sarah all of which he also told he loved and then he had sex with them. We'll call them Louise, Jill and Mary. Now, Louise had three boyfriends before Bill, but those three boyfriends had three girlfriends. And it is the same with Jill and Mary.

Now when Sarah joins with Bill, she is opening herself up to junk passed through intercourse, not just from Bill, but also from Louise and Louise's former three boyfriends and all of Louise's former boyfriends' former girlfriends, and the same with Jill and Mary and all of their former partners. In one night with Bill, Sarah is getting exposed to the physical diseases and contaminations passed through sex from many, many people, a literal sewer.

Let's just compare it on a very small scale of a toothbrush again. Bill is giving Sarah a toothbrush that had been used by 40 or 50 people, some with diseases. Most recently it was used by Bill, and Louise, Jill and Mary, they used it after it had passed from many, many other people.

My daughter Joy is a nurse, and she has informed me there are approximately 31 different kinds of sexually transmitted diseases. Not just the few we hear about most. More than 65 million Americans have an STD, with 20 million new cases being reported every year. STDs are serious and need to be treated, some cannot be cured and are deadly. But the physical body isn't all that is contaminated through sex sin.

The Soul Realm

Now let's talk about the soul realm. I recently heard a teaching by an exciting Christian speaker and author named Kat Kerr. She is a delightful lady with pink hair. God has given her revelation on how our souls have been created. She said our soul has many, many layers. Every layer looks like us, kind of like a transparent image of us. She says we are kind of like a book with pages and every page looks like an image of you. That is how she describes our soul. We have many parts.

We learn in scripture that we become one flesh, with our spouse. This is part of marriage. It is done in love, we take on a layer of our spouse's soul, and they take on a layer of ours and we become one flesh. But like in our scripture, in Corinthians 6:16 we are told that he who unites with a prostitute {or a boyfriend, or girlfriend} becomes one with her in body. That is because they are each taking on a layer of the other one's soul. Those who practice illicit have layers of their soul deposited in many places. There are many deposits from many partners also in their own soul. Their souls are being shattered. Many sex partners literally shatter one's soul.

The good news is through the redemption of our souls through the blood of Jesus, and prayer, which this lovely woman, Kat Kerr does everywhere she goes, you can be set free from these ungodly deposits in your soul and from your soul. As she prays for people, she literally sees in the spirit realm, layers of people's souls coming out of people and returning from other people, reversing the damage done by sexual sins. But the body and soul aren't all that is affected by sex sin.

The Spirit Realm

Now let's talk about the spirit realm. Something similar happens there. It is called transference of spirits. I read a book one time by a man named Bishop Earthquake Kelley called, *Bound to Lose, Destined to Win.*

Bishop Kelley had been chosen as a small child by his evil father to become a voodoo priest. He was trained in the demonic realm and saw what happened in that realm. Even before he got saved, and he did get saved, he would never have illicit sex. He saw what it did in the spirit realm.

He says in his book, **"Through my voodoo training, I already knew about transference of spirits, and I knew the kinds of spirits that attach themselves to people who have sex outside of marriage. Even as a sinner, I wanted no part of that. I had enough problems, and I didn't need to be possessed by any of those demonic spirits."**

In a similar way that disease is spread through illicit sex, demonic spirits are also passed from partner to partner causing spiritual bondages. This man, Earthquake Kelly, who wasn't even a Christian yet, in fact he was living an evil lifestyle, but he understood spiritual things, he was so repulsed by the spiritual garbage passed through illicit sex that he would have nothing to do with it!

Sex outside of marriage makes a big mess on three levels, physically, emotionally and spiritually. I wanted to come down hard on this sin and pull off the deception that it is no big deal. God's way is the only way to avoid trouble. Following His design protects us from much trouble. We need to cherish our marriages and pass the test of faithfulness. {If we have failed in this way it is time for repentance and prayer and time to be restored by the blood of Jesus.}

So many in the past have failed this test and ruined their whole lives. Huge ministries have fallen when the pastor falls into this failure, everything they have built goes down the drain. Not just ministers but politicians, actors, doctors, those from every walk of life. They ruin their careers and then face public humiliation.

And then there is the most devastated of all, the family. How many children have literally had the ground torn out from under their feet, devastated by the selfish acts of a parent whose sin changes their lives as they know it. Only someone who has gone through this as a child can comprehend the devastation.

This sin is not "no big deal" as is portrayed on television. Millions and millions have fallen for this sin and faced some kind of loss, many have lost everything.

Our whole town was devastated a few years back when two prominent men here ended up dead, over adultery. A man known and well liked in our community killed his wife's lover and then himself outside a downtown restaurant. Her lover was her boss, another prominent business owner in the community. Children were left fatherless, and this woman was left with neither her husband nor her lover.

This sin is a wrecking ball leaving its devastating effect on families, children and communities all through history, and even causing death, physical and eternal.

A Conversation with an Angel

My daughter Joy recently had a conversation with her angel about ahem….{sex}. She said her angel never really said the word. But she told Joy something so precious it made me gasp when Joy relayed it to me. She told her when a married couple comes together it cannot be seen in the spirit realm to the angels or spirits. The Holy Spirit covers the husband and wife. He covers them with a canopy that is a green color, kind of like a mist. It is green because it represents the garden of Eden and the purity in which God created marriage. Sex inside of marriage is holy to God and protected.

Sex inside of marriage is very beneficial. It is the opposite of illicit sex that causes damage to the soul. It can bring healing to the husband and wife. It is pure and blessed. Joy's angel also informed her that this green canopy does not happen when an unmarried couple comes together. There is no covering by the Holy Spirit, and they are uncovered and open to the demonic realm. And the demonic realm loves to pervert sex and make it totally different than what God created it to be.

Valuing your Marriage

Of course there is much more to passing the marriage test than just staying faithful, and staying free from sex sin, much more. A few years ago, my daughter, Joy went to the wedding of her friend Daisy.

Daisy is in her forties and has children that are almost grown. We were surprised that Daisy was getting married because she had only known the groom for a month or two. I couldn't attend the wedding, but Joy went and at the dinner she sat next to a woman she had never met. Joy was surprised to find out the woman sitting next to her was Daisy's new husband's ex-wife. The woman told Joy, "We woke up one morning and decided we were both bored with our marriage. We decided we wanted to try something else, we weren't angry with each other just bored. So, we divorced but decided to stay friends."

Joy was aghast. Now this woman was watching Daisy marrying her husband and she didn't seem very happy at all!

This couple did not value their own marriage! It blows my mind how ridiculous this is. It would be like building a house for twenty years and then deciding you did not like the color you painted it, but instead of repainting you just burn the house down!

I can't be too hard on them though, I remember a time in my marriage I decided my husband, Jim, was boring. For several weeks my thoughts had been going that way. My husband was just plain old boring. I thought I knew everything about him, and he was blah. Satan was planting these thoughts in my mind, and I was feeding on them. I was stuck with a boring man.

God did not allow those thoughts to continue very long. Like usual when I start going astray God has a plan to get me back on course.

During my 'boring husband' phase we attended a party at my husband's sister's house. My husband was seated a way away from me having a conversation with a friend of his family. My husband almost never talks about his past. On this day he and this friend were talking about the Detroit mafia. In my husband's younger days, he was mentored by a mafia boss, I knew very little about it and I still don't know much.

I strained to hear Jim's conversation. I was learning things about him I never knew before, things about organized crime and his past. It was more than interesting. It was exciting and scary. I realized something; Jim wasn't boring; he was fascinating. I realized he has been through a lot in his life. He had never been boring. I was the one who was boring.

Thinking your mate is boring is telling you something about yourself. You aren't getting it, this marriage stuff, you are getting too self-centered. My husband has a saying he always would say to our kids whenever they would complain they were bored. He said, "You wouldn't be bored if you weren't so boring." I think it might be true. My 'boring husband' phase was really my self-centered phase. I was focused on myself and Jim not making me excited. That is just all wrong. That is not what marriage is all about. I wouldn't have been bored if I hadn't been so boring! God has made each of our mates and they're extremely valuable, complex and fearfully and wonderfully made.

Giving not Getting

Marriage is not about what you get, it is about what you give. That took me years to get, years and years. Passing the test of marriage begins when your whole motivation becomes about loving this person you are married to no matter what.

I knew an older couple; I met them on my job as a home health aide. The husband was a perfect example of what I am talking about. He passed the marriage test with flying colors. He crossed over to that place I am talking about when it is no longer about you.

This man's name was William and His wife's name was Betty. They were in their late sixties, maybe early seventies; I am not sure exactly. Before I ever even met them, Betty had a stroke. She could no longer talk. I used to go sit with Betty once a week for several hours so William could get out. He usually rode his motorcycle and went to an elementary school where he was a volunteer. He was pretty hip. He had a beard and wore a leather vest. That was his outing, spending time with the school kids.

I never could figure out if Betty could understand a single word I said. If she could, she never showed it. She just stared. If I put a crayon in her hand, she would scribble. I never heard her utter a single word. She just stared with big blank eyes.

If anyone had a right to be bored in their marriage it was William. It seemed like the woman he married was gone. She no longer existed.

But William wasn't bored. He loved Betty. He adored her. It wasn't about him; it was about her. This, very vibrant, interesting and active and lively man, would lovingly care for her. He talked to her just as if she knew what he was saying. He doted on her. He cared for her tenderly. He would dress her and feed her and fuss with her hair. He usually would braid it. And he would kiss her, on the lips.

He always made sure to have a meal ready for me to feed her while he was gone, and a snack. I was to read her magazines and play her favorite television shows. Obviously, Betty was meeting none of Williams's needs; that was no longer possible. But William's love for Betty did not depend on what she could do for him. Marriage to him was about what he could do for her. And everything he did, he did with love.

He got it!!!!!! He passed!!!! He passed the marriage test with flying colors. He put so much value on his marriage that even though he would never again in this lifetime even get a smile from Betty, he wasn't bored, his love for her never even wavered.

Our Biggest Need

I was driving home from work the other day and had the radio on the Christian channel. A talk show called Focus on the Family was playing. They had a special guest who was talking about marriage. What he said was amazing. He said his motives were wrong when he married his wife, he married her for her to fill, what he thought was his biggest need, and that was to be loved. But he has since learned that his biggest need is to learn how to love, and that is how he sees it now. His wife meets his need to learn how to love, not to be loved. It has changed the way he treats her.

Now, I am thinking back to the story about Bob Jones and what he saw in his near-death experience. Jesus standing before us asking us, did we learn to love? What an important question. It was the only question Bob saw Jesus ask. Maybe our biggest need really is to learn to love others. Maybe our mates are God's answer to that need. Could it be that the focus of our marriage is to be not on receiving love but giving love? Could that be how we pass our marriage test?

Yes! Yes! Yes!

Chapter Nine

The Test of Forgiveness

And when you stand praying, forgive, if ye have ought against any: that your Father which is in heaven may forgive your trespasses. Mark 11:25

Forgiveness may not seem like a test we have to pass but it is. Many have failed life and eternal life because they have refused to forgive. They become bitter. A root of bitterness grows in their hearts, an ugly evil root, and it destroys their relationships, their health, their outlook, and if left it can destroy their eternal soul. Many have gone down to eternal doom because they did not pass the test of forgiveness.

God has commanded us to forgive. If He commands us to do something, then it becomes possible to do it, even if it is impossible, because if He commands us to do something, He will help us to do it. This is something we have to do to pass the test of life so let's just make up our minds to do it and that is that.

Those who forgive are just the opposite of those with the root of bitterness in their hearts. They have not blocked the flow of God's blessings and they are blessed because of it.

You might think that I could not possibly know the pain or hurt that someone has caused you. You are right. I do not. But in order to be free you have to forgive. And in order to be forgiven you have to forgive. Some have had to forgive more than others. Some have had to forgive others for unthinkable horrors. It has to be done.

Summer's Struggles with Forgiveness

I have had several instances in my life where I have tried to forgive people and I just couldn't. Neither of the people were sorry and both of them continually opened the wound before it could heal.

The first one was the man who broke up my parents' marriage. As hard as I tried to forgive him I couldn't. He was in my life now like a huge dark storm. Every time I tried to forgive him, he wreaked more havoc and caused more pain, sinking me deeper into grief and making it impossible to forgive him.

I tried for a year, crying myself to sleep every night, trying to forgive him, but couldn't. God stepped in and took it away. It was a miracle, and it was a lasting miracle. One minute I hated him and the next minute I didn't.

It happened like this. I had made an effort to go to see him and my mother, although it was tense and uncomfortable. My feelings toward him hadn't changed. I still loathed him. My mother also felt the tension and she was chatting away nervously. I barely heard her. While she was chattering, he muttered something under his breath that struck me funny, and I started to laugh. I laughed the rest of the day.

I knew God was doing something; he healed me through the laughter. The hatred left me permanently. The amazing thing was this man was still on a path of destruction and continued to hurt my mother and my sisters. He even stole the money out of my purse one time several years later. But the hatred never returned. I just kicked myself for being stupid enough to leave my purse in the room that he was in. The anger never returned. In fact, I prayed for him for years and rejoiced at the fact that in his later years before he died, {young} that he seemed to turn his life around. It felt so good to be free and to be free enough to be able to care what happened to someone who hurt me more than any other person on earth.

Years later I had another issue with someone who hurt one of my children and continued to twist a knife into my child for many years. God did not miraculously take this one away. As hard as I tried, every time I saw her cause my son pain, it hurt. My son was ground to dust. When someone hurts your children, you want revenge. You want God to immediately strike them dead with a lightning bolt.

I could not seem to pray for God to bless her or her family, who I felt, were equally responsible, because I didn't want God to answer my prayers and bless them. I did not WANT them blessed!!!!! I was hoping God would just miraculously take away the unforgiveness like the last time. He didn't. After years of struggling, this time God gave me a strategy instead. He said, "Try remembering her the way she used to be."

It worked. If I thought of her a prayer would go up. If I thought of her family a prayer would go up. I would have small setbacks because the situation is still the same, but I would remember my strategy from God and pray for not only her but her whole family. I saw them differently.

It feels good to pray for those you used to hate! It is like kicking the devil a good one in the shins! I am all for that.

Consistent Forgiveness

Marriage takes consistent, continual, persistent, constant, forgiveness. I wasn't used to having to forgive so much when I got married. Not only that, but I also knew I was never wrong, and everything was his fault. I was totally self-centered. So not only did I have real things to forgive him for, I had perceived things to forgive him for. Tthen throw on top of all of that my husband was an alcoholic and sometimes used drugs. I had trouble, trouble, and more trouble.

For so many years anything I reached out for seemed to be snatched out of my hand by alcohol. I was constantly frustrated and angry. It was never ending.

I never ever had enough. There was not enough money to pay the bills or for groceries. I would long for a bottle of shampoo, or money to go to the laundry mat. I would see my sister get new clothes; I wanted new clothes. I wanted my little boy to have toys. He had almost no toys.

One time I got my son a little bouncy horse at a garage sale. I was thrilled and he was thrilled. He bounced for days he loved his horse. It didn't last long; Jim in a drunken rage smashed it to pieces. I was angry, angry, angry! I thought if he would quit drinking all my problems would be over. I would beg him to stop. And Jim would agree he would promise to quit, and it would sometimes last, for a short time.

Every time he would start drinking again, I would have to forgive him, but I was devastated every time. Extremely devastated. Terribly devastated. I kept hoping for a life and it kept getting snatched away, I would see light at the end of the tunnel, and it would get snuffed out. I wanted out of poverty. I wanted security. I wanted peace and happiness and safety. I have had to learn to forgive, consistently, continually, constantly and completely.

So now, all these years later everything is different now, right?

He never drinks now, right?

And everything is normal, right?

Well no. {We talked about this in an earlier chapter.} He has had long sober periods but recently he has had a major setback. He is in trouble again, because of drinking and having a setback in his mental health. I don't know what the future holds again. All of a sudden, I am back in the same boat.

So, have I forgiven him?

Yes.

Am I still so angry?

Actually, I am not. Am I going to leave my husband?

No never.

Is it still so hard? Do I have nothing and is everything miserable? Actually, it is not. Why?

Something has changed since those early years. I see things differently. I am thinking more about him and less about me. My life has not been a piece of cake, but something wonderful happens when you pass the test of forgiveness, something very wonderful. God steps in. God steps in and He does something amazing. First, He makes everything okay. He somehow puts the pieces back together every time they fall apart.

Now I reach out and God gives me miracle after miracle after miracle after miracle. Alcohol no longer seems to have the power to destroy my life. My life is in God's hands. I wanted a house for so long, but like everything else I wanted that seemed impossible.

I love my big, beautiful house. Yes, despite of no money and a drinking husband I have a house, a big house. It was a miracle how we got it.

All three of my children have college educations, another miracle. I have a car that runs! A good job! A pool in my back yard! Five wonderful grandchildren! You can't believe how God blesses me! His flow is no longer blocked by anger or unforgiveness. I no longer reach out and have nothing; I reach out and receive.

I also want you to know something else. It totally devastates me when my husband drinks, but I forgive him.

I have forgiven him for years. I know I must. I am not angry with him. I am not hurt. I am not holding onto anything he has done. I feel no regret. And I have had to forgive him again and again and again. I have forgiven him, I love him. Sometimes he promises me he won't drink ever again; he swears up and down and tells me not to worry and two hours later I smell it on him.

And I want you to know something else too. I did not do it well, but I did do it. I did learn to forgive, but that is no reflection on me, I did not do it well. I have gone through such anger. I have screamed at my husband; I have screamed at God. I have cried, mourned, begged God to kill me, begged God to kill my husband, been angry, been sad, been depressed, wouldn't put up a fight, then put up a fight, I have opened the cupboards and smashed all the dishes, tore my wedding picture off the wall and smashed it, I have even landed in jail, I know what angry is!

But I have managed to forgive, yes, but it wasn't easy, and I am no saint. But I am free through forgiveness.

An Amazing Woman

I recently read a story about a woman whose life is a testimony to forgiveness. I enjoyed every word of this book because I so related to this woman who was married to an alcoholic and what she went through. This book amazed me. I want to tell you about it. It was called, *The Prize Winner of Defiance Ohio,* by Terry Ryan. It is a memoir written by a daughter about her mother, Evelyn

Ryan, an amazing woman.

Evelyn Ryan had her hands full, she raised ten children, and her husband was an alcoholic. Because of her husband's drinking, Evelyn's life was a real challenge and money was a huge issue, because a large portion of her husband's salary was spent each week on liquor. Evelyn did not focus her life on her husband and what his behavior was doing to her family, she never got bitter.

She focused on writing jingles and poems. Back from the late forties to the early sixties most contests put on by companies were actually contests of skill requiring contestants to send in jingles. Evelyn supplemented her family's income with the jingles she sent to contests and poems sent to newspapers.

Her daughter writes of seeing her mother standing at the ironing board with a pencil behind her ear and a notebook at the end of the board, writing jingles while she ironed. Then after dinner she wrote her jingles until she fell asleep on the couch.

In 1953, when the family, then eleven of them, were being evicted from their two-bedroom rental home, Evelyn won a big prize and won $5000. She used it for a down payment and moved her family into a four-bedroom home. The timing was unbelievable. The book tells of the struggles Evelyn has, and how she perseveres with such an indomitable spirit.

Once she won a ten-minute grocery shopping spree. She mapped out the grocery store planning the food she would grab in her timed food grab. Her problem was the small carts that the stores had back then, they didn't hold many groceries. She talked it over with the butcher the night before. He solved her problem he cut and wrapped her some tall flat meat cuts to put all around the shopping cart which made the sides of the cart much deeper. She also enlisted her troupe of kids to watch the time and keep calling out how many minutes she had left so she could keep up with her schedule. The shopping spree was scheduled before the store opened in the morning. When the man with the stopwatch yelled go, Evelyn sprinted through the store like an Olympic athlete. All in all, she netted $411.44 worth of food, about $3000 worth by today's standards.

Through the years Evelyn was awarded cash and prizes which brought hope and courage to her children. She won televisions, bikes cars, a freezer and washer and dryer, and clocks. Also, her poems, that were printed in papers would bring in anywhere from one to twenty-five dollars. She kept her family going.

But her biggest test came when the phone rang one day, it was the bank. Her husband had taken out a second mortgage on their house four years earlier and had never told her. Now the money was spent and $4000 was due in thirty days or they would lose their house.

Things looked hopeless. She begged the bank for a payment plan, but they refused. They could not even scrape up $100, let alone $4000. Things looked hopeless for all of them. This was the worst thing her husband had ever done and this time it looked like the end of them. Evelyn started to make plans for where her children would go if they lost their home.

Evelyn received a miracle just before they lost the house. Days before the bank deadline Evelyn received a phone call telling her she had won a big contest, the last big one she'd ever win. She won the grand prize in the Dr. Pepper contest. She won a trip to Switzerland, {which she traded for cash} a new car, $3440.64 in cash and his and hers gold watches. It came just in time for her to save her house.

This story just absolutely amazed me! Who gets miracles like that? I believe Evelyn tapped into miracles because of her attitude. She did not focus her life on the abuse from husband. She did not allow herself any self-pity or depression. She focused on what she could do for her family and that was writing jingles and caring for her children and husband. She opened herself up to God's miraculous flow by refusing to block it with anger and bitterness.

As I read this awesome book about his amazing woman, I scoured the pages for some clue or secret to how she kept going through such adversity with such courage and hope. There wasn't much, but there was a paragraph or two when her daughter, the author was venting her frustration to her mother one day about how unfair things were. And she was frustrated that her mom hadn't won a contest because she thought her mom's entry was so much better than the one that won. Her mother could sense a deeper frustration and gives her daughter some wisdom. It gives us a peek at Evelyn's secret to success. I will quote the book.

"I don't know," I said frustrated. "I just think

those guys are wrong to say your entries aren't good enough. I know your entries are better than good. One of them should have won something!"

"Are you sure you're just talking about contests?" she asked. "Remember; these judges are professionals—they're hired to judge my poetry or jingles and that's okay. But I have a feeling you're talking about another kind of 'judge'—people out there who think they can pass judgement on someone like me and you and that's not okay."

"You mean--"

"I mean some of our neighbors, or the police, or Father McCague, or a few of the nuns at St. Mary's. They think we're lesser people because we don't have a lot of money. Do you agree with them?"

"No. You know I don't care about them."

"Remember when the nuns at St. Mary's thought you were dumb? You went on to prove how smart you were to the teachers who really count didn't you?"

"Yes, but Mom! We should have told those nuns off! They pushed us around and we never did anything wrong! It's just like—just like—"

"Just like what? Like Dad?"

I jumped up. "Yes! Just like Dad! They're all like Dad! Why don't we ever get to stand up to Dad?"

Mom nodded as if she had been waiting for this question for a long time. "Because, Tuff, 'standing up' to your dad would mean nothing. In fact, you'd be wasting your time and energy you should be spending on your own life. You could spend hours every night fighting with

Dad about whether he's being 'fair' to us ---or you could do what you're doing: getting good grades, planning for college, saving your own money."

We both sat at the table now, looking out the window into the yard. "Sometimes I hate him, Mom."

"I'm not surprised. Considering what we all go through every night, it's normal that you would. But try to think harder about what you really hate."

"What do you mean?"

"A long time ago I figured out something that made life a simpler. Don't let yourself be judged by others, and don't judge other people."

"Someone judged *you*?" I said, "Why?"

"It doesn't really matter why," she said, "and it was a long time ago. But it sure made me think twice before judging any-one else, including your dad. I don't even like to judge my own contest entries. I like the feeling of being actively engaged in something that might one day bring in a little cash."

This gives us a little clue about Evelyn. She is a free woman. She is free from bitterness and free to be creative and focus on her own life. She has not blocked the life-giving flow from God by anger, bitterness or negative emotions. She is an example to all of us.

God wants us free. He wants us free from unforgiveness and bitterness and any other negative emotion that blocks us from His love and His provision and His constant blessing flowing into our life and through us. This woman kept herself free and God was able to super naturally provide for her. Her story is miraculous.

Forgiveness can really be tough, but it has to be done. It is a commandment, a requirement. But it is life changing and worth it. The benefits are enormous; we are open to receive God's blessings and provision. Our forgiveness defeats our enemy, Satan. It is hard, believe me I know, but it is a test we must pass.

Chapter Ten

The Test of Thankfulness

In everything give thanks; for this is the will of God in Christ Jesus for you. 1 Thessalonians 5:18

Giving thanks in every situation is God's will for us. That does not mean that you are thanking God for the situation, you are thanking Him in the situation. This powerful principle is life changing. This is the proper response for the good things and the bad things that happen to us. It is the response of faith.

An Army Chaplain Discovers Praise

In the 1970's a military army chaplain named Merlin Carothers discovered the power of praising God in any situation and he wrote the book *Prison to Praise*. Merlin was taught this principle by God.

Merlin was noticing in his Bible how many verses in the Bible that told us to rejoice and be thankful in everything. When God asked Merlin if He was glad that Jesus suffered and died on the cross for his sins, Merlin said he was. Then God told Merlin, "Now listen, my son. For the rest of your life when anything happens to you that is any less difficult than what they did to My Son, I want you to be just as glad as you were when I first asked you if you were glad Christ died for you."

Merlin agreed to give thanks in everything. But the next morning he forgot when it was time to get out of bed and he sat on the side of the bed wishing he could go back to sleep. God quickly reminded him he had promised to be thankful for everything. As he continued to go through things that normally irritated him, God continued to remind Merlin to thank Him for everything.

Then one day when Merlin's car wouldn't start. Merlin again was put to the test. Merlin continued thanking God. Merlin headed for the repair garage on base but when he got there the on-duty mechanic told him the mechanic who worked on his kind of car was in the hospital and he would have to take his car to a civilian repair shop. The mechanic also told him the civilian repair shop had been taking advantage of the situation and overcharging everyone from the base who had brought their car there.

Merlin continued to thank God as he pulled into the car shop; he was remembering what God had told Him to do. The mechanic at the civilian shop refused to give him a price and said it may take a while to fix his car. Merlin agreed to bring the car back the next day. He struggled to start his car and then start pulling out when the mechanic called for him to wait, "I think I might know what the trouble is," he told him and worked under the hood for a moment. "Try to start it now," the mechanic said as he finished. Merlin started the motor and this time it purred like a new car.

"How much do I owe you?" Merlin asked surprised.

"Nothing," the mechanic replied.

Pulling out of the shop God spoke to Merlin again, "My son what I wanted you to know was that you never have to worry whether anyone will overcharge you or mistreat you unless it is my will. Your life is in the palm of My hand, and you can trust Me for all things. As you continue to thank me in all circumstances you will see how perfectly I will work out every detail of your life."

Merlin continued thanking God for everything. When he thanked God for his regular migraines they never returned, the same for his allergies. Soon he started to tell others that came to him as chaplain to do the same. The results were amazing.

A young soldier, named Ron came to Merlin in desperation. He wanted Merlin to talk to his wife. Ron's wife, Sue, had tried to commit suicide when he joined the army and now that he was being sent to Vietnam she threatened to try again if he left.

"What can I do," Ron asked. Merlin agreed to see her. For the rest of the story, I will quote the book.

Sue was also a picture of misery. Her body was frail, and she sat on the edge of a chair, trembling from head to foot. Tears flowed uncontrollably down her face.

"Chaplain," her voice was barely audible. "I'm scared; I can't live without Ron."

I looked at her and a wave of compassion brought tears to my eyes. I knew Sue's story. She was adopted as a baby, was estranged from her adopted family, and had no one in the world except Ron. The two of them were very much in love and I knew if Ron went to Vietnam, Sue would stay alone in a rented room in a strange town.

I prayed silently for wisdom to comfort her.

"Tell her to be thankful." I shook my head in disbelief. I must have heard wrong.

"Her, Lord?"

"Yes, you may begin with her!" I looked at Sue's tearful face and my heart sank. "Okay, Lord, I trust You."

"Sue I am glad you came," I said smiling with a confidence I didn't feel. "You don't have anything to worry about. Everything is going to be all right. "

Sue straightened herself, wiped away her tears, and managed a trembling smile. I continued: "What I want you to do is to kneel here with me and thank God that Ron is going to Vietnam."

She looked at me in blank disbelief. I nodded. "Yes, Sue, I want you to thank God."

She immediately began to weep almost hysterically. I calmed her as best I could and began reading to her from the Bible verses, I had learned to trust over the past few months.   ". . .In everything give thanks for this is the will of God in Christ Jesus concerning you. . .All things work together for good to them that love the Lord." Carefully I tried to show her the wonderful truths I had found to be real.

Nothing seemed to help. Sue believed in God and in Christ, but in her despair her belief was of no comfort. Finally, she left my office crying, with no peace of mind and certainly no joy.

"Lord, have I completely misunderstood you? The girl wasn't helped a bit."

"Patience, son, I'm working."

The next day Ron came into my office. "Chaplain, what did you tell Sue? She is worse than she was before."

"I told Sue the solution to her problem and now I'll tell you. I want you to kneel down and thank God that you're going to Vietnam and that Sue is so upset she is threatening to kill herself."

Ron didn't see my point either. Carefully we went

over the scriptures: ". . . This is the will of God concerning you." Ron said: "Now I understand why Sue didn't understand, I don't understand either." And he left.

Two days later they came back. "Sir, we are desperate. You must do something to help us." They were both hoping that I as chaplain would be able to put in a plea for another assignment for Ron.

Again, I explained to them the only solution God was letting me hold up before them. "All things work together for good to them that love the Lord."

"If you can only believe that God is really working this thing out for the best for both of you, then all you have to do is trust Him and begin to thank Him— regardless of what the situation looks like."

Ron and Sue looked at each other. "What do we have to lose Honey?" Ron said. They knelt and Sue prayed: "Lord, I thank you that Ron is going to Vietnam. It must be Your will. I sure don't understand but I'll try."

Then Ron prayed: "Lord, this is very strange to me too, but I trust You. Thank you that I am going to Vietnam and that Sue is so upset. Thank you that she might even try to hurt herself."

I had a feeling that Ron and Sue were not as convinced as I was, but I thanked the Lord that they were trying. They left my office, and later I heard what had happened.

Ron and Sue had gone into the chapel and knelt together at the altar. There they had turned their lives and each other over to God in a new deeper commitment than ever before and now Sue had strength to pray: "God, I thank You that Ron is going to Vietnam. You know how much I will miss him. You know I don't have a father or mother or brother or sister or family of any kind. I will trust You, Lord," Ron prayed: "God, I thank You. I give

Sue over to You. She is Yours and I'll trust You to take care of her."

With that they rose from the altar. Ron went through the chapel and headed for his unit while Sue came back to the waiting room next to my office. She needed to sit quietly and collect her thoughts. While she sat there a young soldier came in and asked for the chaplain. Sue told him that I was busy. "But if you wait a little while, I'll tell him you're here," she offered.

"I'll wait," said the young soldier. He looked distressed and Sue asked: "What is your problem?"

"My wife wants a divorce."

Sue shook her head: "It won't do much good to see *that* chaplain," she said, but the soldier wasn't easily discouraged, and while they were waiting, he took out his billfold and began to show Sue pictures of his wife and children. When he turned to the next picture Sue screamed: "Who is that?"

"That's my mother."

"That is *my* mother," said Sue shaking with emotion.

"That couldn't be," the soldier replied. "I don't have a sister.

"It is; I know it is!"

"What makes you think that?"

"When I was a little girl, I happened to find a piece of paper in my parents' desk that showed I was adopted. In the upper right-hand corner was a picture of my real mother. That's her. It's the same lady."

And it was. Further checking revealed that Sue had been promised for adoption before she was born, and her natural mother had never seen her. She had no idea where Sue was and had never heard anything about her since the day she was born.

Now Sue had a brother, a real brother, and with him came a whole family. But that wasn't all. Ron walked back into his unit; he ran into an old friend from law school who was now a legal officer.

"Hi, old buddy, where are you going?" he said as he met Ron.

"Praise God, I'm going to Vietnam," Ron answered. They talked some more, and the friend persuaded Ron to ask for a transfer so that he could work with him in the legal office.

Ron and Sue did not have to be separated. And no longer did Sue have to cling to Ron in fear of losing him. She had come to have a joyous confidence in Jesus Christ and went about everywhere praising Him.

This story is miraculous. You would hardly read something so amazing in a fiction novel, let alone a true story. Living God's way is better than fiction! Thanksgiving opens us up to His miracles. His miracles can be beyond belief!

Merlin Carothers books on praise have sold millions of copies, and he has become a voice to the body of Christ on this subject. I remember reading them with my mom and sister. We loved his books so much we read them out loud together. I am glad we did because through the years I would remember the lesson learned and use it.

It Works

There was about a seven-year period in my adult life when my family went through extremely hard times, especially financially. I never seemed to have enough money for groceries to eat, so other things that were bought at a grocery store I just had to do without, little things like shampoo or Q-tips or band aids etc. We had to save our money for food.

I remember wanting a bottle of shampoo. Our neighbor would bring over her paper after she read it and I cut out a shampoo coupon. I waited until triple coupon day at the grocery store and bought the smallest size bottle of shampoo. It was Prell. It only cost me about thirty cents. I was thrilled to have my beautiful little bottle of shampoo. It was green gold. I used it carefully so it would last. I loved my little bottle of shampoo!

Well, bath time was our nightly routine at my house. It was more like our fun. I would put my one-year-old daughter and three-year-old son in the tub every night about seven, before bed and they would play for forty minutes or so.

Well, shortly after I had purchased my little bottle of green shampoo while I was getting the one-year-old daughter out and dried off I turned around and my three-year-old son had dumped out my bottle of shampoo. There was only a tiny bit left.

My heart sank. How could I have been so stupid to leave it on the side of the tub? You cannot believe the loss I felt over that bottle of shampoo. It depressed me. I felt like my whole life was going down the drain.

Whenever I tried to get ahead a little something worse would happen and everything was always going down the drain. I felt like for years every time I reached out my hand for something good it was snatched away just like my bottle of shampoo and this bottle of shampoo was the straw that broke the camel's back. It was just too much.

I knew I didn't have money for another bottle of shampoo, and I lamented to God. Suddenly I thought of Merlin Carothers books and thanking God for everything. That was a lifetime ago when I still lived at home and my parents were still married and I wasn't, and life wasn't a constant trial.

I said a prayer, "God, this seems like a total waste, but I know you can take any situation and use it for good. So, I thank You and I praise You that my bottle of shampoo went down the drain."

I felt better. I didn't know how but I knew somehow something good would come out of this.

I didn't have to wait long. My husband worked as a janitor at a small college. A couple of days later he came home with a bag of something. He said, "I was cleaning out the lockers and someone had left this in there. I didn't want to throw them away because they are almost full."

I looked in the bag, it was a large bottle of shampoo and conditioner. I let out a squeal. It was a great big "I love you" from God to me.

Not only was it a bottle of shampoo but also a bottle of conditioner!!!! It was like getting a dozen roses sent from heaven! But God wasn't done yet. My sister came to the door a day or two later. She and her husband were moving away. She said I don't want to move these it's not worth the bother and she handed me another bottle of shampoo and conditioner.

"Are you sure?" I asked. I couldn't imagine

someone giving away something that was such a luxury.

After she left, I had to sit down. It was like another dozen roses from heaven. God can make good from any situation!

But God wasn't done yet. My dad and his fiancé came down to see me. He had a big bag with him. He said, "We are changing to a certain kind of shampoo, so we are getting rid of all the old bottles we had. There were about six or seven bottles of shampoo in the bag!

After years of shampoo being a rare luxury, I had a whole cupboard full of shampoo! It lasted me a year and a half! I could wash my hair whenever I wanted! I felt like the God had opened heaven and poured out shampoo all over the place!!

This thankful stuff works!!!

I have to tell you I can afford shampoo now; those days are over. I keep extra of everything. I have about three bottles of shampoo right now. I usually have about seven bottles of laundry soap and the same for dish soap. I keep cupboards full of extra food. My mother comes over and gets after me. You have too much food! But I like it this way.

Thankfulness a Way of Life

I have used this principle many times in my life when I have felt a sense of loss, but I feel like God is revisiting this principle of thankfulness and saying, "Make this a way of life."

It is time to start living this stuff we believe, not

just once in a while but every day, in every situation. This is a test. It is a new level of trust in God. It also helps us learn the lessons He is teaching us. I believe that gratefulness is the key to happiness and contentment. I believe it is a key to getting closer to God and experiencing heaven on earth. David wrote in the Psalms that we enter His gates with thanksgiving, and we enter His courts with praise. Let's begin to give thanks in everything!

I want to live this way. I want to pass the thankfulness test.

Chapter Eleven

Retaking Tests

My brethren, count it all joy when you fall into various trials, knowing that the testing of your faith produces patience. But let patience have its perfect work, that you may be perfect and complete lacking nothing. James 1:4

When my daughter, Joy was in Bible School, she told me her instructor said, "There is no failing God's tests, you just keep taking them over and over again until you pass."

Have you ever noticed that you go through the same things over and over? Then it could be you are retaking a test. I have a friend named Mary who found this out. Mary's first marriage ended in divorce. She married again hoping this marriage would work, but it didn't. She said husband number two was just like husband number one. Now she was divorced again. She decided never to marry again, she'd had enough, her children from the first marriage were older now and she thought she would just make it on her own.

Sometime later a man named Bob from Mary's church asked Mary out for dinner and although she wasn't interested in him, she decided to go. "I just wanted a free meal," she told me.

Later that night, after the free meal, while she was home in bed, the Lord spoke to her in a radical way. He told her, "Bob will be your husband." Then she had a vision, she saw Bob and her getting married the vision even continued on to see Bob and her having children together. They were old enough to be grandparents. When Bob called her again and said, "I think God wants us together."

Mary answered, "I know."

Mary and Bob did get married, and they had two children together. Mary was always one to obey God; she was the one of the strongest Christians I had ever met. I looked up to her in every way.

Naturally I assumed that given the dramatic way that God put Bob and Mary together that the marriage was pure bliss. But that was not so. Mary said that if she hadn't known God put them together it never would have lasted. She told me Bob was the same personality type that her first two husbands were and that she found herself right back in the same situation as the first two husbands, difficult.

It was from Mary that I learned that God puts us in situations for a reason. God was perfecting Mary through her husband. She thought all her husbands had personalities that were incompatible with hers, but that was not the case, God was tempering her through marriage. {Just as He does with a lot of us.}

You will be happy to know Mary passed the test on her third try. She also stuck it out and became very happy with Bob. There are some tests you are going to just keep taking over and over until you pass them. Many times, people just want their life to be comfortable. Anything that makes them uncomfortable they weed out of their life, whether it is a husband or relative or situation. They don't want anyone to upset their applecart. The problem is it is not God's agenda to give them an easy life. His agenda is to grow them up into a mature child of God.

God Will Bring Down Our Idols

People make idols out of anything, money, houses, sports, pets, their lawns or gardens, even their carpet. God sends the carpet worshippers dirty little feet to help Him do His work.

I remember reading a story one time in a magazine. The writer was a man, named Alex, who was writing about the summer when he was just a boy that his neighbor, Mr. Johnson hired Him to water his rose garden while he went away for several days. Of course, Alex was thrilled when his mother told him Mr. Johnson called and asked if he would like to earn some money. Alex thought this would be easy money, just watering his neighbor's roses.

Mr. Johnson's roses were quite a sight to behold. They were his pride and joy. Everyone in town talked about Mr. Johnson's roses and he seemed to spend all his free time working in his rose gardens that went all around his house.

Before Mr. Johnson left, he called Alex over to show Him how carefully he must water his roses twice a day and using the utmost care.

Alex got up early the first morning and watered Mr. Johnson's roses, then off he went to play baseball with his friends. Alex lost track of the time playing ball with his friends as he walked home, he suddenly remembered Mr. Johnson's flowers. "What could it hurt just to miss one watering," he thought to himself, and he headed home.

The next day as Alex headed for Mr. Johnson's place his friends called out for him to come join them. He thought for a moment, looking over at Mr. Johnson's roses, they looked okay. So, Alex once again ran off with his friends.

Alex told himself that night that the first thing in the morning he would do was water Mr. Johnson's roses. But the next morning Alex put it off again thinking he'd be sure to water the flowers after the game.

Alex felt guilty all through the game. This time he couldn't get Mr. Johnson's roses off his mind. As soon as the game was finished Alex went running to Mr. Johnson's house, but it was too late. There was Mr. Johnson, and his roses were ruined. Alex looked in horror and Mr. Johnson was crying!

Alex felt terrible. When he got home his mother was waiting for him and Mr. Johnson had called her. Alex hung his head down in shame.

As time went by Alex tried to forget his failure to Mr. Johnson but it was a burden he carried around. Several years later, and older now, Alex decided he must go and apologize to Mr. Johnson. Nervously Alex went to see him. As he apologized, he did not get the response from Mr. Johnson he expected.

"You actually helped me Alex," Mr. Johnson said, "You see I had made those roses the most important thing in the world to me. When the roses were destroyed, I realized how unimportant they really were. I need to thank you."

This story really impressed me. Alex was actually being used by God to help Mr. Johnson base his life on something more important than roses. Our lives need to be founded on the Rock, our Rock, Jesus Christ.

If we are idolizing something in our lives, we can expect God to send us an Alex to bring our idol down. We will face the same situation over and over until we learn the lesson we need to learn, like Mary and her three husbands. God is bringing situations into your life for your own benefit, to grow you up and mature you, and to weed out the things in your heart that are holding you back.

God Upsets Our Applecart

I once knew a good Christian couple with four children. They so wanted to protect their children from worldly influence, so they homeschooled all of them. The problem was they insulated their children from problems. Their children were in a bubble, they were not learning to handle problems; they didn't have any!

God sent them help in the form of a holy terror. The couple's nephew was having problems at home, so they decided to take him in. When their nephew came, he really upset the apple cart. He drove them all nuts. The couple, thinking this wasn't good for the children, sent their nephew back to his home.

God spoke to me about this family. He said, "I sent that boy to this family to minister to them. He is exactly what they needed. They keep taking themselves out of the situations I am putting them in. So, I am going to put them in a situation they can't get out of."

Troubles and trials can actually be good for us if we learn what we are supposed to learn from them. We can't keep taking ourselves out of the situations God is putting us in to mature us. The Bible says, the testing of our faith produces patience, and when patience is complete, we will be perfect and complete lacking nothing.

In other words, finally we will have passed the test.

Chapter Twelve

Reducing the Problem the Key to Passing Tests

For many years to make a living I used to run a newspaper route. I would deliver papers, between four and five hundred papers every day. They had to be delivered by six a.m. Sometimes I would need some help. Sundays were hard, especially near the holidays. Sometimes I just didn't feel good and there was no such thing as a day off. I worked three hundred and sixty-five days a year, rain or shine or hurricane. {We lived in Florida}

One night I decided I needed help and decided my son, Jamie, should help me. I told him he was going with me that night and to be ready; I would wake him to go about one thirty in the morning.

Jamie was about nine or ten years old. He was my oldest, so I thought he was the best bet. When I went to wake him up that night, I couldn't get him roused. He didn't want to wake up, he wanted to sleep! I finally got him up and dressed and, in the car, but he was angry, tired and grumpy, all three. We got to the substation to pick up the papers, but Jamie wouldn't get out of the car to help. I had to wake him up again but still he wouldn't get out of the car to help. He sat in the car angry with his arms crossed and refused to move. No matter what I tried he wouldn't speak to me, and he wouldn't move.

The Real Issue is You

I realized he was tired, and he was young, but he also had an important lesson to learn. We were a family and a pretty poor one. We needed this money to live on. I had to do this every day whether I felt like it or not and I needed some help. His dad could not come because he had to work in the morning and besides, we needed an adult home with his two little sisters. I knew it was hard, but I also knew he had to do it.

I got in the car and had a talk with him. I told him, "I need help, but this is also about you. Forget about these papers and this night and me and everything around you. Take all this stuff away and there is just you and God. This all comes down to you and God. These papers and all this are what God is using to teach you. But right now, you need to forget about everything but you and God. That is what is important. If you are going to get up and do what you know you are supposed to do. The time, the place, the situation is not important what is important is you and

God. Are you going to do what is right?"

I got out of the car, and I started folding the papers. I left him in the car to think. And I started thinking too. "Where did that speech come from?"

I started to realize what I told Jamie was true. The important thing was not the papers getting delivered. Oh, it seemed desperately important at the time. I needed my job to pay my bills. But I started to see something deeper. Jamie was the most important thing in this situation, his inner man, the type of character being built in his heart.

This physical world and all its situations and changing scenes are not the real issue. The real issue is us and God. The situations are here for us; to test us and to help us and not to help us get the temporal thing we want NOW. No, these things around us are only shadows, they pass, and their importance passes. We are the important thing that doesn't pass. The real value can't be seen because the thing of utmost importance to God is us and the eternal work He is doing in our hearts.

God is using these passing scenes to develop our eternal character. For some the situation might not be helping their mother deliver papers, the situations are endless. For some, like Joseph, it may be an injustice. For others it may be a betrayal from a friend, or a loss of a job, or let us say a sibling that has stolen your inheritance. How are you going to respond?

The important thing is not the inheritance, it is not the money! No matter how important it may seem to you the real value is YOU, how you respond. Yes! How you respond! It is between you and God. How will you respond? Respond to please Him! It is of infinitely more value than your inheritance, or in Jamie's case his sleep, that thing you want. It is hard to see that now because it is something invisible, but it is real. God is doing a work an eternal work and the finished product is YOU!

Make every situation about you and God! Simplify it. Take away the papers and the night and the car, just you and God. Take away the passing scenes of this life, money, objects, anything that seems important; get it down to you and God. Am I starting to get through? Are you starting to get a little glimmer of what I am saying? Everyone's situation is different and yet everyone's situation is the same. There is a test to pass.

A Man's Test at Work

For some it may be a situation at work, someone who is being mean. How are you going to respond? Remember it is not about the situation it is about you and God. I want to quote a man's testimony about this very thing. I read it in a wonderful book called, *How to See in the* Spirit, by Michael R. Van Vlymen. He had to learn the same lesson.

At one time in my life, I was given a boss who was mean, rude, ill-tempered, deceitful, and those were his good points! You can imagine! I would go to work and he would brow beat me in front of people, threaten to fire me, find ways to make me work "off the clock", and so on. My prayer for him was, "Lord please let him not suffer to much as a bus runs him over." I had no love for

him. But what I failed to consider was the fact that God is not willing that *any* should perish. He loved this guy! And He wanted to save him!

One night I was in my prayer chair, asking God for deliverance from this ungodly man and the Lord spoke to me, "I want you to bless him," is what the Lord said. I wasn't really on board with that, but I began anyway, "Lord, bless him with salvation and bless him with deliverance, save him from hell." Not a real enthusiastic offering.

The Lord spoke to me again and said, "No, bless him as if he was your son." Well, if he was my son I would definitely pray differently. So, I began. It took me a little while to really feel sincere, but I blessed him in every way I knew how. I blessed his life. His family, his finances and everything else I could think of. I gave him two and a half hours of my undivided prayer time.

When I was done, my spiritual eyes opened, and an angel of the I Lord showed up and gave me a small gift. It was a gift that signified that I was justified now through faith in the word of the Lord. He had told me what to do. I did it in faith even though I didn't really understand why I had to do it. But God blessed me.

And I also found out that my boss no longer had any hold on my life or my emotions. The Lord had set me free. Then, on top of that, two weeks later he was fired. The Lord moved him out of my life. I think that if perhaps I had interceded for this man three years earlier, I would have saved myself a lot of grief.

After three years Michael passed this test. After

three years he made it between him and God. He responded the way God wanted him to. Michael passed the test and then God removed the test because he passed it.

I once heard Rick Joyner, my favorite author and founder of Morning star Ministries say something very interesting. He was coming under heavy criticism from another ministry. He prayed and asked God, "Please stop them from criticizing us"

"Well, who would you like to do it?" the Lord replied.

These are tests! Make them about you and God. Respond the way God wants you to respond and PASS them. Start stripping away the earthly things or situations or people that you are facing and reduce your situation to the lowest common denominator, you and God. Now solve the problem. Respond the way God wants you to respond. Remember your response is the most valuable thing in each situation. Look at the invisible, the eternal, not the temporary. You are being tested. You are what is important. You growing up and maturing and becoming like Christ.

As I stood at my car folding papers, Jamie came out and stood beside me. He was still tired, but he began helping me. He helped me all that night and other nights too. He passed his test.

Chapter Thirteen

"There Are Worse Things than Dying"

For scarcely for a righteous man will one die; yet perhaps for a good man someone would even dare to die. But God demonstrates His own love for us, in that while we were still sinners Christ died for us. Romans 5:7-8

"There are worse things than dying." I got that line from a western movie called *Open Range*. Actually, the line was more like, "There are worse things than dyin." Read it with a western drawl. The whole movie was worth watching just for that one line. It stood out to me. The movie was about a town that one evil rancher and his hired bad guys pretty much ran. The town's people lived in fear but didn't stand up to them, and the sheriff was just another bad guy employed by the evil rancher.

Then some brave men, passing through with their cattle, had a run in with some of these bad men who, for no cause, killed one of their friends and wounded the other. So, the two cowboys that were left then stand up to the whole bunch of the bad guys. Standing up for what was right, against so many, was almost certain death, and no one in the town dares to stand with them. That is when the cowboy says it, "There are worse things than dyin." And what he meant was for him to allow evil men to kill and do nothing about it; that was worse than dying. Next comes a big gun fight with a lot of action, the two brave cowboys face death and save the town. Now everyone is safe.

What are the worse things than dying? Is it possible that some will face tests that could possibly cause them to risk their lives or even lose their lives? Are there tests that are so important that passing them is worth losing your life? Yes, yes, yes, what is worse than dying is failing the test! How could any test be that important?

Following Jesus' Example

Jesus faced huge tests. One test required Him to fast forty days and face Satan in the wilderness. And of course, His last test required Him to face mocking, scourging, torture, death and hell, the lowest pits of hell. He overcame. It was His purpose and He passed that test and it has reaped eternal rewards, unspeakably holy, magnificent, unimaginable, eternal rewards. We think we understand the outcome of that one act, but we don't, and we won't in this lifetime. The treasures of salvation are vast, and they are endless. We have all eternity to discover them, but for now, we take it by faith, and we follow Christ's example. There are worse things than dying.

Heroes of the Holocaust

World War 2 was a time of unbelievable evil. It was as if hell came to earth. I have read countless books and accounts of World War 2. It is unthinkable to me how such evil was carried out by human beings on other human beings.

It started slowly and escalated. Jewish children were beaten at school, by children who had been their friends. The terror continued, the Jews were set apart, they had to wear a star on their clothing and were put in ghettos to live. Race riots were encouraged; Jewish homes and businesses were broken into and ransacked. Jewish men were beaten, and many killed.

That was the beginning of the horrors. Soon they began putting people in concentration camps. Many times, they would separate the families and take the children out and immediately kill them with machine guns and then take the parents to work camps which later became death camps and few survived. Two thirds of Europe's Jewish population were killed, roughly six million people. There were other people targeted also, handicapped, homosexuals, and mentally ill were a few. All together with the Jews, eleven million were killed.

Many of the pictures I have seen of this time shows humans, the Jewish people, almost always completely naked, and they look like skeletons. It was so horrible it is beyond my imagination and yet it really happened.

And yet there were those in the midst of this horror that stood out from the madness. Those who risked their lives or paid their lives to save those they could. World War 2 brought out those who would rather face great loss and death than turn their backs and allow this to happen.

One man was actually a Nazi himself, Oskar Schindler, who saved 1200 Jewish people during the war. This man was no angel, but he could not allow innocent people to be killed. He kept the Jews who worked in his factories alive by paying bribes to SS guards and by feeding them from the black market. This man who spent the first part of his life in the pursuit of wealth, eventually spent every last penny he had, and risked his life, to save the Jewish people employed by him. When faced with the test of his times, he passed. He saved the people that he could, even though it cost him everything.

And there were others like him who passed this test. Another was Irena Sendler, a nurse and a social worker who saved 2500 children by smuggling them out of the Jewish ghettos to safety.

She smuggled children and infants out of the ghetto to safety, by hiding them in the bottom of her toolbox or boxes or burlap sacks in her truck. She then gave them false identities and hid them with foster families and in convents. Irena kept records of the children's identities buried in a jar.

She had a dog she trained to bark when she passed the Nazi guards as she left the ghetto. The dogs barking covered the children's sounds, and the guards didn't want to deal with the dog and would let her through.

Irena was eventually caught and tortured by the Nazi's. They severely beat her and interrogated her. They wanted the names of her coconspirators and her records of the children. But Irena refused them. They broke her legs and sentenced her to death.

She was rescued by friends bribing the guards but was listed as dead. Irena spent the rest of the war in hiding but continued her rescue efforts. After the war Irena attempted to reunite the children with their parents with her carefully kept records, but most of the parents were dead. Irena, like the cowboy, realized there were worse things than dying and she passed her test.

One more was Carl Lutz. He was appointed in 1942 as a Swiss vice consul in Budapest, Hungary. He issued Swiss safe documents that enabled 10,000 Jewish children to emigrate. Then when the Nazi's took Budapest in 1944, and began deporting Jews to the death camps, Carl gained permission to issue 8,000 protective letters for 8,000 Jews to immigrate to Palestine. Carl issued tens of thousands of protective letters to Jewish people all bearing a number between 1 and 8,000.

One day, in front of a fascist militia firing at the Jews, Carl jumped in the Danube River to save a bleeding Jewish woman. He declared her to be a foreign citizen protected by Switzerland and put her in his car and left. No one dared to stop him. He is credited with saving 62,000 Jews! Think of it, 62,000 people were saved by one man who was willing to put his own life on the line for them.

After the war he was criticized by his government by overstepping his authority and risking Switzerland's neutral status. There is something more important than the Swiss government to face and that is an eternal government, God's government. Carl Lutz is one who belongs to that government, because he passes the tests of eternity, the ones that matter.

Many others did similar things during this period. Some paid with their lives. Some we may never hear of, but their deeds are recorded in heaven. All through history there are those who have risked their lives to save others during evil times.

Yes, there are tests that are worth dying for. Tests that prove your worth to God. Tests that may cost you everything, in this life, and maybe even cost you your life, but it is worth passing those tests because," there are worse things than dyin."

Chapter Fourteen

When You Fail

I so so so hate it when I miss it. See, I can't even say it, I mean, when I fail. There have been so many times.

I remember one time I felt God was prompting me to write to a Christian couple I knew from another town. I tried. I started writing to them over and over, I had sheets of paper all over the house with the words written on it, Dear Donna and Joe, that was all, I couldn't figure out what I was supposed to say next, I'd get that far and then blank. After a couple weeks of writing just their names, I just gave up. A short time later I dreamt I was pregnant, and my baby died. I woke up knowing that I had aborted what God was trying to do. I felt a deep since of sadness.

We Can Learn from Failure

Failure can be a learning experience. It feels awful,

it is like repeating a grade in school, but sometimes it is needed, and we learn and grow from mistakes. I have since learned when I just can't hear from God, and I know He is trying to tell me something it is because I am not willing to hear what He is saying. I have learned to let go and get willing to hear whatever He might say. A lot of times it is something I do not want to hear, but once I get willing, then I can hear Him again. I believe this is why I could not write the letter.

A Painful Lesson

I remember another time I really missed it; it still hurts to think about it, but I really learned a lesson. The lesson I learned was to take advice from my husband. What happened was this, early in our marriage we were going through a difficult time financially and I needed a winter coat. We lived in Northern Michigan, and it was winter, it was a desperate need. My husband, Jim and I were walking through the mall, and he saw a sign in the store window for a contest. The winner could pick out any coat in the store.

Jim ran up and filled out a card with my name and stood in the middle of the mall praying over the card. He was convinced this was the answer to my winter coat problem. Sure enough, a couple of weeks later I got a call, I had won the contest.

Jim went with me to look at all the beautiful coats. Jim picked out a nice warm winter coat that would have been a good choice for my needs. I didn't listen to him. I got caught up in the moment and let the sales lady talk me into getting the most expensive coat there, a long leather fall coat.

I was being very foolish. I agreed on the coat she chose for me; they took my picture to hang up in the store and we left. As soon as I got in the car, I realized how stupid I had been, and I felt sick. I needed a winter coat! I got a fancy leather coat for fall. I still needed a winter coat! Jim had been right there telling me, but I wouldn't listen.

When I got home, I called the store and asked them if I could bring the leather coat back and get a winter coat, but they refused. I never wore that coat. I hated it. It was some time before I got a winter coat. I had blown it big time. But I learned something. I was a smug 'know it all' who never listened, because I thought I knew more than everyone else, especially my husband. I learned to listen to my husband's advice. It was a painful lesson.

Failures are painful, I wasted winning a contest, but something bigger was gained here, respect for my husband. Failures are learning experiences, IF, we learn from them, and they can become steppingstones.

The Easy Way or the Hard Way

I want to quote a passage on this very topic from one of my favorite books called, *The Call*, by Rick Joyner. I will have to give you some background. This book is a record of a wonderful heavenly prophetic experience had by the author, Rick Joyner. Rick, in this vision, has fought a great battle with the enemy, with a demonic horde, and climbed great heights on the mountain of God. Throughout this battle and spiritual climb his armor he is wearing has become very glorious and brilliant.

The Lord gives Rick a plain brown robe to wear over his glorious armor. Because of its brightness it is hard for Rick to see. It is the mantle of humility. Rick is almost offended by it because it is so plain. It looks more like something a homeless person would wear. He later learns the robe is what Jesus wore while He was on earth and is highly respected in heaven.

Now in our passage Rick is in a heavenly place, and he is thrilled to be speaking with the apostle Paul. He is wearing the plain, drab, mantle of humility. Paul warns Rick that with all the glory revealed to him he must never take off the cloak of humility. But Rick feels so drab next to the glory of those around him. As he peeks under the cloak, he sees his armor shining gloriously. So, to keep from feeling so embarrassed by the cloak's plainness, Rick makes a huge mistake, he removes the cloak. I will quote the book.

There was silence, and I stood quietly for a few moments. I was unable to see anything because of the brightness of my own armor. I did not understand why I could not hear anything either. I then called out for Wisdom.

"*Put your cloak back on,* " I heard Him reply. I did as He said and began to dimly see the outline of the Great Hall again.

"Lord what happened to everyone? Why is

everything so dim again?"

"You can see nothing here without wearing that cloak."

"But I have it on now, and I still cannot see very well," I protested, feeling a terrible desperation.

"Every time you take off humility you will be blinded to the true light, and it will take time for you to see again."

Even though I was beginning to see the glory again, it was nothing like before. My vision was coming back, but very slowly. I was grieved beyond words.

Where is Paul?" I asked. "I know he was about to tell me something very important."

Jesus who is Wisdom in Rick's vision explains to Rick that Paul left when he removed the cloak of humility, because without it he would not be able to receive Paul's message.

"It is true that you missed an important revelation by taking off your cloak. It would have helped you, but if you learn the lesson not to ever take off the cloak again, especially for the reason that you just did, you will have learned another important lesson."

"Lord, I think I have learned that lesson. I do not remember ever feeling this bad. Can they not come back now and share what they had for me?" I begged.

"All truth and Wisdom come from Me. I speak through people because the people I speak through are a part of the message. While you remained humble enough to keep your cloak on, I could speak to you in My glory, whenever you take off that cloak, you become spiritually *blind and deaf. I will always speak to you if you call on Me, but I must change the way that I speak to you.*

"I do not do this to punish you, but to help you receive your vision back more quickly. I will give you the message that I was going to give you through these witnesses, but it must now be given through your enemies. It will come with trials, and you will have to bow very low to receive it. This is the only way that you will get your vision back as quickly as you need it. For what is coming, you must be able to see."

There is so much marvelous stuff in this passage, especially about humility. But what I want you to glean from this passage is Rick has failed a little test here. He was not to take off his cloak of humility, but he did. Now he cannot hear what Paul was about to say to him. He feels such remorse and loss. I know that feeling! I felt it about that letter I could not get written! I felt it about that coat! I missed out! Rick missed out! But the Lord tells Him if he learns the lesson, not to do that again, he will have learned another important lesson. It is a very painful lesson.

Learning lessons through failures is painful. But if we do learn them, it causes growth. Now Rick will have to learn what Paul was about to tell him with difficulty, through his enemies!!!!

I do not like the sound of that.

And it will come with trials; I really do not like the sound of that!!!!

And he will have to bow very low to receive it!! I really, really do not like the sound of that. This is not taking the easy way; this is taking the hard way! It would have been so much easier to have heard it from Paul.

When we fail our tests, we will still get the opportunity to pass them, but it gets harder the second time around! We can take the easy way or the hard way. Believe me, I have done this, I have taken the hard way, many times.

Summer Took the Hard Way

I will tell you of one time I took the hard way. I talked about this in my earlier book, *The Impossible Marriage*, but I want to talk about it again here because it fits this point so well. I really took the hard way. Back in the years of my husband's heavy drinking, God wanted me to go to AL-Anon. It was a group for the families of alcoholics. I did not go. I didn't want to, and I didn't think I needed it. God really tried to get my attention.

First, we had a special speaker at church that did a lesson on alcoholism and the importance of the families getting help. I still did not want to go. I preferred prayer meetings. Years went by and I did not go. Then one time I was in my favorite prayer meeting, as the leader of the group was praying, she got quiet as she was listening to God and said, "Summer is not supposed to be here, she is supposed to be in the 12-step meeting."

Our church had a Christian version of Al Anon led by a wonderful Christian lady whose husband had been an alcoholic and now she taught a twelve-step meeting. It was on the same night as my prayer meeting. When God spoke to her, my prayer group leader actually got me up and walked me down to the twelve-step class. I only went once. The next week I was back in my prayer class. I did not realize how stubborn I was being. I just did not think it was necessary and I didn't want to go.

I really took the hard way. God gave me time but then He stepped in. He used the law. I have noticed God does this, when we ignore what we are supposed to do, He gets tough.

One night when my husband had been drinking and things got out of hand, the police came and took us both to jail! I was ordered by the court to go to AL Anon meetings. I had to bring a paper to each meeting to get signed to prove that I had been there, which I found very humiliating. Guess what I finally went, I had to; I did not want to go back to jail. I had to go to several meetings a week for six months. I could have taken the easy way. I could have gone to the much more pleasant meeting that met at our church, no jail, no papers to sign, but I wasn't listening. I took the hard way.

There are times when we fail our tests. It is a horrible feeling, but if we learn our lesson, it is still an important lesson learned. We will still have to pass our test, but it may not be as easy this next time around. Like Rick, and me, we may learn from our enemies, and we may have to bow very low to learn it. {Believe me, I like the easy way better!}

Chapter Fifteen

The Good the Bad and the Ugly

For to be carnally minded is death; but to be spiritually minded is life and peace. Because the carnal mind is enmity against God: for it is not subject to the law of God, neither indeed can be. So, then they that are in the flesh cannot please God. Romans 8:6-8 KJV

In our last chapter we talked about failing tests. The biggest lesson we can learn from failing tests is to stop failing tests. Those who continue to go their own way through life and ignore God's warning signs are heading for serious trouble. They are like a speeder who is driving down the road of life ignoring all the traffic signs. Recklessly they continue driving in the wrong direction. They come to a warning sign that says **Do Not Enter, Danger Ahead,** but they continue on. God continues to warn them that they are racing to their own destruction. He puts roadblocks in their path; He puts up more warning signs. There are flashing lights and sirens in their rear-view mirror. He arrests them. Many will stop and take correction. They turn around and get back on the right road. But some continue on crashing through every roadblock until their road abruptly ends and they go crashing over the cliff into the bottomless pit of destruction where the wrong road leads, eternal loss.

God's Ways of Turning Us Around

God usually takes a similar plan with all of us, like He used with me. First, He speaks to our heart. He tells us what to do. For me it was Al Anon, but for some it may be a wrong relationship they are flirting with, which may lead to an adulterous affair. For some it may be an addiction like drugs, alcohol, gambling, smoking etc..

God deals with us gently. He uses the still small voice in our spirit to lead us and direct us away from danger and to the right path we are to take. If we continue going the wrong direction, He will speak to us in other ways.

There were many times I have gotten on the wrong path. One time I was going the wrong direction in my life. I started sinning and I knew it was wrong. During that time, I fell down the stairs and sprained my knee. I knew God was speaking to me. I knew what I was doing was wrong and believe me I straightened up quick. It was a spanking and it worked.

He has done many things to get my attention. One time He had my car roll into the street from my driveway. I looked out of the window and traffic was stopped. There was my car in the street all by itself. It had rolled back from my driveway. As I ran out to move it, I felt extreme embarrassment. I knew God was showing me if I continued on the road, I was on that time that I would be humiliated. I straightened up quickly again. God will speak to us in many ways, to turn us around.

If we still ignore God, He will send someone to speak to us. Like in my case, when I was ignoring God about going to AL Anon and He had my prayer leader speak to me and she even walked me to the twelve-step meeting. At this point He will send someone to warn you.

God has used me in this way too and has sent me to warn others a time or two. Believe me I did not want to do it, but I did. I felt I was not good enough to tell someone to change. Once I had to speak to a father who was being too hard on his children. Another time it was a young woman who decided sin was better than serving God. God told me firmly, when I balked; if He tells me to speak to someone, I had better do it. I have had them listen and I have had them not listen.

If we continue on the wrong path, we are in serious trouble. The next step is more severe. He may arrest us; in my case it was literal. We will be publicly humbled. In my case I was dragged out my front door in handcuffs and put in the back of a police car in front of my gawking neighbors. I was locked up in a jail cell, it was no fun!!! And then I was ordered by the court to do what God had been telling me to do all along!

In the case of adultery, you may be caught, exposed and humiliated. Depending on your circumstances you may be exposed some other way, the loss of a job, etc... God is trying to get you off this road that leads to your destruction. Now He is using more extreme methods. He sees where it leads. It is time to wake up! We can stop at any time and turn around. God will continue to deal with you more severely hoping to turn you around before it is too late, before we run out of roadblocks.

Some Lessons Learned from a Book

I want to tell you a true story I read one time. Reading the story was a gentle rebuke from God. He was showing me where the path I was on could lead me. It was about food. I was addicted to ice cream for years. I literally had to have it. I would crave it so bad I would run to the store just for ice cream. I would eat so much of the box that I would not want my husband to see how much I ate so I would finish off the box so I could throw it away before he got home. I was an ice cream addict.

Back to the story, I love to read. I have read many books about people's experiences during World War 2. World War 2 was a time of extreme tests in many people's lives. This particular book was about a young girl, named Marie, who lived in Germany during World War 2 and two incidents in the book really stood out to me.

The first incident was earlier on in the war, because she lived in the city and situations were harder there. She had an opportunity to stay out in the country with a woman, named Helga. Marie's pastor was contacted by Helga because she wanted to help a young girl get out of the city into a safer environment. The pastor thought of Marie, so Marie was sent to stay with Helga her benefactress.

During the war food was rationed, only a certain amount was allotted to each person. With Marie present, Helga was allotted extra food for Marie's needs.

Soon, young Marie found out the real reason Helga had invited her to stay. Helga was a glutton. She wanted more food. Every day Marie received less and less food. All the while, Helga was reminding her of how much she was doing for her and how grateful she would be. As Helga got greedier and greedier, Marie got to the point she was literally starving to death.

One of Marie's friends at school, who realized how hungry she was, would share her lunch with her at school. Otherwise, she was getting nothing to eat, and she was getting weaker by the day. Finally, Marie was able to get word to her pastor who came and rescued her before she starved to death.

Helga allowed her lust for food to take her to the lowest point. She was actually killing a young person, so she could eat more, all the while, telling herself and everyone else she was helping her. Didn't she have any conscience left as she watching this young girl starving to death, just so she could stuff more food into her mouth? Food had become her god.

I put down the book and gasped. Suddenly gluttony did not look like a harmless little sin to me anymore. It looked very ugly. I decided my ice cream eating had to come to an end. I did not want to become another Helga.

I continued to read Marie's story and something else stood out to me in the book. Later in the story, when Marie is a bit older, her mother becomes ill and has to stay in the hospital. While Marie's mother did receive medical care, the hospital did not have sufficient food to feed her. Marie's mother depended on Marie to bring in food to feed her.

Marie, out of great love for her mother, stopped eating and brought her mother all her food during this time. Surprisingly Marie found a miracle taking place. All the time she gave up her food for her mother she never lost weight, or she never felt all that hungry. God was giving her a miracle! As she out of love was sacrificing her food for her mother, God was supernaturally, feeding Marie.

I had to put the book down in absolute amazement. I had to stop and think about this and try to figure it out. Marie was supernaturally, being fed by God, when she out of love sacrificed her food for her mother. But Marie almost starved to death several years earlier when she was used by Helga to feed her gluttony. Why was that? Why didn't God supernaturally feed her then?

I came to realize something. God has given each of us real power in our lives. We have the power to do good or to do evil. We are not puppets that God uses and always determines the outcome. Our lives affect others. But we are responsible for our actions. Helga chose to allow her appetite to bring her so low that she would kill an innocent person to eat. Unless she repented, she has an eternal destiny awaiting her in hell. Maybe the embarrassment of her motives being discovered turned her around. I don't know, we can only hope. God allows her to choose her own destiny. I am sure she passed many roadblocks as she continued her destiny down the wrong path, but she ignored them.

God did save Marie and she escaped death, but not without first suffering at Helga's hands. Helga will have a real punishment to pay. Many suffer or even die in this life, at the hands of those who choose the path of wickedness like Helga chose. They do real damage, but they will pay the consequences.

On the other hand, God did a miracle for Marie as she fed her mother. The right path, the path of love, the path that Marie chose, the one that would lay down one's life for another is the path of life, the path of miracles and the path of eternal rewards. I learned a lot from reading Marie's story. A lot about passing and failing the tests in our lives.

God will help us if we listen. But He has given us a free will. He will allow us to continue on the wrong path if we choose to ignore Him. He will speak to us. He will try to get our attention. He will send others to speak to us, He will put up roadblocks. He will arrest us and allow us to be humiliated. But if we still harden our hearts and continue down the wrong path, we will end up where that path leads, to loss or worse yet, destruction.

Chapter Sixteen

Regard for the Weak

Blessed is he who has regard for the weak; the Lord delivers him in times of trouble, The Lord will protect him and preserve his life; He will bless him in the land and not surrender him to the desire of his foes. Psalm 41:1-2

Defend the cause of the weak and fatherless; maintain the rights of the poor and the oppressed. Rescue the weak and the needy; deliver them from the hand of the wicked. Psalm 82:3-4 NIV

How you treat the weak of this world has extreme importance. It will determine how God treats you. Because in essence how you treat the weak **is** how you treat God. He tells us that in His word. I will give you a few examples.

He who is kind to the poor lends to the Lord, and He will reward him for what he has done. Proverbs 19:17

Then the righteous will answer Him, "Lord, when did we see you hungry and feed you, or thirsty and give you something to drink? When did we see you a stranger and invite you in or needing clothes and clothe you? When did we see you sick or in prison and go visit you?" The King will reply, "I tell you the truth whatever you did for one of the least of these my brothers of mine you did for Me." Matthew 25:37-40 NIV

God takes what you do for the weak personally. It is the same as doing it to Him. God forbid that you should take advantage of the weak! He takes that personally also. If you want to please big daddy God in your lifetime, then let's help the weak. Let's talk about who are the weak.

The Poor

I know all about the poor because for many years I was the poor. I hated being poor! Believe it or not, people take advantage of the poor. Our society oppresses the poor. Banks oppress the poor. They charge exorbitant overdraft fees when poor people overdraft their accounts causing them more financial stress.

I knew a young family who was struggling financially. They over drafted their account by just a few cents. The bank sent them a letter which took a couple of days for them to receive it. By the time they got the letter the bank had charged them $180.00 in overdraft fees. I went with the young woman to see the bank manager to try to get them to remove the fees. He would not budge. Now they had a huge debt to pay. I was so angry at his lack of concern for the poor. They also charge the poor higher interest.

And it is not just the banks either, if someone gets behind on a utility bill they pile on the fees. The poor pay more for insurance too. We are not to make a profit off the poor!!!! Just the opposite we are to help the poor. I remember in some of my husband and I's most desperate times when my husband was unemployed and needed work, being scammed by ads in the paper. Employment agencies promising work and charging a fee and they had no work to offer. They were just making money off the desperate.

We are not to oppress the poor. Let's read our scripture again, *Proverbs 19:17 He who has pity on the poor lends to the Lord, And He will pay back what he has given.* We can see in this verse how personal God takes it when we give to the poor. I found it out firsthand.

When our family used to live in Florida, I got very used to seeing people with signs that said, **WILL WORK FOR FOOD.** I usually ignored these people, especially after a friend of mine who had a business tried to give a man who regularly stood on the corner a job. The man told her to get away from him; he made plenty of money holding that sign. I also felt that I shouldn't give able bodied men money when I was struggling to feed and clothe my own children.

One day I broke my rule. I had just picked up my husband, Jim, who worked at the mall. We were at the light at the exit of the mall. That was a favorite spot for the men with the signs because we all had to stop right in front of them and wait for the light to turn green. This particular day there was a man with a sign that read, **HUNGRY, VIETNAM VET.** He pulled at my heart. I feel this country owes a debt to the Vietnam vets and I could not pass him by. I found two dollars in my purse and asked my husband to hand it to the man. Jim said to me, "You'll just waste your money; he will just go buy booze with it."

"Maybe not," I said, "he looks hungry and he's a vet."

So, my husband leaned out the window and handed the guy the two dollars. As the man thanked Jim, Jim said to him, "There is a McDonalds behind you go get a hamburger."

The man replied to Jim, "I need to save it for cover, someone stole my cover."

Jim leaned back in the car and told me, "He's not hungry you probably bought him booze."

I didn't know if I did the right thing or not. I soon found out I did. Later that day I went to the grocery store. As I came out of the store, I noticed a cart sitting all by itself with a gallon of milk in it. I knew it wouldn't last long in the ninety-five-degree sun but still I was just going to leave it there. I thought whoever left it will probably come back for it.

The Lord spoke to me, "Take that milk, no one is coming for it."

I picked up the milk and put it in my car and the Lord spoke again. "A gallon of milk costs two dollars; I just paid you back for the money you gave the homeless man."

I realized I had done the right thing. God had rewarded me. We need to realize how important the poor are to God. When we help them, we are literally lending to the Lord!

The Elderly

It is a good thing for all of us to show regard for the elderly, because guess what? Someday it will be you! Do not honk your horn at them when they are driving slowly! They have to drive slowly because their reaction time has slowed way down, and they cannot handle driving fast.

Elderly people need help. They can't keep up anymore. They need errands run and chores done. They need help to go to the doctor and the store and to church. They need things fixed. You will get more than God's blessing when you help the elderly, you will get wisdom and perspective that is beyond your years from the elderly. It will help you to see how soon life is all over and what is really important in life. Something we can't get sight of when we are younger. Helping the elderly is another way to honor God.

The Sick or Handicapped

Of course those who are sick would fall under the category of the weak. The sick and the handicapped are in such a humble position. They need help with their most basic needs, such as eating or going to the bathroom, or bathing. We can't imagine how that feels. Many in nursing homes have been subject to abuse because their needs are so great.

I saw a movie called, *The Drop Box* the other day. It is about a Pastor in South Korea who put a box in front of their house, so that mothers' can drop off their unwanted babies in it. The box is like a huge, oversized mailbox and it has a bell. The mother places her child in the box and rings the bell. Day or night when the bell rings the pastor gets up and rescues the baby. There was a need because babies were being discarded on the street and were being found dead.

The Pastor is a little grey-haired man named Pastor Lee Jong-rak. The thing that absolutely amazed me about this film was the way the children were treated. Many of these children have extreme handicaps and yet they are adored and lovingly handled, at a level I had never seen before.

In a newspaper quote, it says of the handicapped children he cares for, "One is deaf, blind and paralyzed, another has a tiny misshapen head. There's another with Down syndrome, another with cerebral Palsy, still another who is a quadriplegic, with permanent brain damage. But to Pastor Lee Jong-rak they are all perfect. And they have found a home here at the ad hoc orphanage he runs with his wife and a small staff."

The movie I saw, *The Drop Box,* was made by a young college student named Brian Ivie, who went to Korea to make this documentary.

Brian said, "I wanted to see where the love came from." Love, the love comes through in the documentary. That is what amazed me so. I never saw such love. The Pastor looked at and held each child, whether they were handicapped or perfect, as if he was holding a priceless treasure. There was lots of hugging and cuddling. I could see the peace in the handicapped children's eyes as they were lovingly held and fed and washed.

Not only were the adults loving and kind to the children, the children, were loving and kind to each other. They were acting out the love given to them. As I watched this movie, I thought that these people were the godliest people I had ever seen in my life.

Brian Ivie came back to the States and changed forever. He had gone wanting to become rich and famous with his documentary, but he returned a Christian. In his book, *The Drop Box: How 500 Abandoned Babies an Act of Compassion and a Movie Changed My Life Forever,* which Brian has written since he returned, he writes a letter to Pastor Lee Jong-rak. I will quote it.

Pastor Lee,

Thank you for showing me your life before God, so I could finally understand where the love comes from. Thank you for never taking the glory, even when you stay up all night and destroy your own body to save the cold, little ones that might be left outside. And thank you for getting up every time the bell rings.

Do you think Pastor Lee Jong- rak has passed the test of life?

Children

Children are on God's list of special people and especially the orphans. Just because someone is small and weak does not make them unimportant. No, it is just the opposite, because they are extremely important to God and that makes them extremely important.

I remember three little boys in our neighborhood who were three holy terrors. They had a reputation for being wild and unruly. They lived just around the corner from my house and right next door to my best friend, Rhonda's house. I saw them often and many times in my backyard, because the oldest boy, named Chris, was my son Jamie's age, about ten years old. They would play together.

Wherever the oldest boy, Chris was, the two younger boys were also. The youngest was barely older than a toddler. All three boys were always together. You see Chris had to keep an eye on his younger siblings. Their parents never seemed to be around, and the responsibility of his younger brothers fell to Chris. I never saw one, but I saw all three. Even though these boys had a mother and a dad they seemed like orphans. Rhonda, who lived next door, told me their parents would come and go as they pleased, never giving a thought to their children.

I would sometimes cringe when I saw them in my backyard, wondering what would be broken when they left. One day one of the boys, I think it was the middle one, hit our dog, Sam, in the head with a baseball bat and split his tongue. Poor Sam, for the rest of his life he had a split tongue. That only made me cringe more when I saw these boys coming.

During this time my son Jamie became an avid baseball card collector. Every penny he got went to buying cards for his collection and because his dad, my husband, Jim, was on board with his hobby. Often when Jim came home from work there was a pack of baseball cards in his pocket for Jamie.

Jamie had quite a collection going, it was impressive. But Jamie's most prized cards were his Will Clark collection. He kept them separate. Will Clark was his favorite player. His Will Clark cards were kept together in a special album.

One day after Chris and his brothers had been around and left, Jamie became distraught. His Will Clark collection was missing. We looked everywhere but it was gone! To Jamie this was devastating. Jamie was in tears. I felt horrible for him. I knew how hard and how long he had worked on this collection. This was his most prized possession, and it was gone. Jamie and I both started to wonder if Chris took it. In fact, we became convinced Chris took it. I thought to myself that is the end of his cards. As wild as those boys were, I figured those cards were gone for good.

I was wrong.

Jamie called Chris and asked him if he had seen his cards.

About ten minutes later we heard knocking at the back door. In all the years we lived in that house it was the only time there was ever knocking at the back door, that backyard was completely fenced in.

The whole family went to the back door to see what was going on. There was a tearful Chris standing at our backdoor holding Jamie's Will Clark collection. It was late and it was dark outside, and it was the only time I had seen Chris without his brothers.

"I am so, so sorry," Chris stuttered, "I don't know why I took them." He was shaking and he was barely looking up. And he just kept apologizing over and over.

I was speechless. I stood there in awe. I was sure Jamie's cards were gone forever. All Chris had to do was lie and say he didn't take them, which is what I thought he would do. In fact, if I was his age that is probably what I would do. In fact, I might still do something like that now if I made a mistake and didn't want to own up to it.

But he didn't. This rag tag ten-year-old, with way too much responsibility shoved on him and little to no parenting given to him, didn't lie.

I could understand why he took the cards. He had very little, and he had no dad helping him with such things. It was unattainable for him.

What amazed me was that he brought them back!

This boy, who was used to disapproving glances given to him by the adults in his neighborhood because of the reputation of terror he and his brothers had, came and faced us. In fact, he marched himself over to our door and faced our entire family, alone! On his own accord he apologized and returned the baseball cards!

I stood there astounded. I was so moved I couldn't speak. I was actually in awe at the character of this ten-year-old waif. He had more courage and character than most adults. I know he had more courage and character than I did. I would not have been that brave.

Jamie was elated to get his cards back and grateful. He pulled Chris into the house and took him into his room. Chris left with plenty of baseball cards that night, just not Jamie's Will Clark collection. Jamie gave him other cards that didn't mean so much to him.

When Chris left our house that night he was smiling. But when Chris left our house that night I was changed forever. My heart was cut. I realized I had wrongly judged this ten-year-old boy. I thought he was trouble. But I was wrong. I needed to look past the gruff little exterior and see the heart of this child.

This child had shown such character. A child so alone with so much responsibility displayed more character than most adults. He certainly gained my respect. I never saw him the same way again. He not only changed the way I looked at him, but he also changed the way I looked at everyone. It is character that matters, and this child, this holy terror, had more character than most people. I don't ever want to judge someone like I judged him again. I couldn't have been more wrong.

Chris was weak and vulnerable. He was only ten and his ten years had been difficult. He didn't have a dad that collected baseball cards with him. He didn't have adults that nurtured him and loved him like most kids do. There are many Chris's in this world. We have to look past the rough tough, rag tag exterior and give them our regard, and to help them. This is no small thing. To do so is to touch the heart of God.

Those in Prison

God's attitude toward those in prison is not that they deserve to be here and that got what was coming to them. NO! It is just the opposite. God is closer in the prisons than he is in most churches. His Spirit is there. His heart is there. Wherever the hurting are, God is there. Again, God wants us to remember those in prison.

Remember, we are not capable of judging another human being. Only God sees the heart of a person. Only

God knows how difficult a person's situation may be. Prisoners to God are like buried treasure. The treasure is the souls who have been cast off by society. That is God's favorite kind of treasure. We see a lump of coal and God sees a diamond in the rough.

Of course, you want to use discretion; these men aren't locked up because they missed Sunday school.

When my husband, Jim, was in prison he was very lonely. The things that meant the most to him were mail and a visit. Also, the PTL Club sent Jim a Bible which he cherished.

Any person you see in a weak and vulnerable position, what you do for them you have done for God.

Is this not the fast I have chosen: To loose the bonds of wickedness, to undo heavy burdens, to let the oppressed go free, and that you break every yoke? Is it not to share your bread with the hungry, and that you bring into your house the poor who are cast out; When you see the naked you cover him, and not hide yourself from your own flesh? Then your light shall break forth like the morning, your healing shall spring forth speedily, and your righteousness shall go before you; The glory of the Lord shall be your rear guard. Then you shall call, and the Lord will answer; you shall cry, and He will say, 'Here I am.'
Isaiah 58: 6-9

Chapter Seventeen

Pick up your Garbage!

I went by the field of the slothful and by the vineyard of the man void of understanding; And, lo, it was all grown over with thorns, and nettles had covered the face thereof, and the stone wall was broken down. Then I saw it and considered it well: I looked upon it and received instruction. Yea a little sleep, a little slumber, a little folding of the hands to sleep: So, shall thy poverty come as one that travelleth; and thy want as an armed man, Proverbs 24:30 -34 KJV

I know a woman who has been leaving her garbage around for years. She rents an apartment and never cleans it. She never cleans the fridge, and it gets moldy, she doesn't take out the garbage and it piles up and she doesn't clean. The place gets totally trashed. She also doesn't pay the rent and eventually gets evicted. She leaves the landlord out thousands of dollars, first in unpaid rent and then in clean up and damage.

She has followed this pattern over and over in her life. When she could no longer rent an apartment, family members tried to help her. She treated her family members the same way, even her own parents. Everyone who has tried to help her has had to clean up destroyed property. She is not only leaving a physical trail of garbage for others to clean up, but also a financial pile of garbage as well. She is not alone, there are many people going through life leaving a trail of garbage behind them, some of it is seen and some of it is unseen.

Being Responsible

Cleaning never came easy for me either. I was nineteen when I got married and moved out of my parents' house. After a week or two every dish in the house was dirty. When there were no more in the cupboard, I realized I had to wash the dishes. There was no dish fairy coming, it was me or nothing. It never occurred to me for quite some time to wash the dishes after each meal. I waited until every dish in the house was dirty and then I would wash them, and it would take several hours. I was beginning to realize that things were not going to get done unless I did them; I was supposed to be responsible now.

Soon a baby came along. He needed to be fed every few hours and about every hour or two his diaper needed changing. He even got wet and got hungry in the middle of the night! I had to wake up and I was tired! I was the one who was supposed to do this; I had no fairy godmother waiting to help me. I had to be responsible. My time was no longer my own to do with as I pleased. More babies came and more responsibility. More than I seemed to be able to handle. I think there were several years that I never saw the bottom of the laundry pile and when I finally did get to the bottom, the clothes had molded.

I was incredibly irresponsible and suddenly I have all this responsibility. I had to grow up. I still couldn't quite figure out how to keep a house clean. I tried. I remember the Lord actually had to speak to me and tell me how to clean. I was trying to clean, and I was just going in circles. I had some soapy water and a rag. I would start to wash a wall and then I would see something across the room and start doing something else and I got nothing done.

The Lord stopped me. He said, "Start with one thing and finish it. I want you to take you bucket and rag and wash all the windowsills." I did it. Then He had me wash the living room walls, one thing at a time. I had been a housewife for years, but I never seemed to be able to keep things clean. The Lord's method worked, one task at a time, I got better.

My husband opened the stinky fridge one day and had enough. My mother cleaned houses for a living and my husband paid her to clean out our fridge. I was insulted, humiliated and appalled. After all I would every once in a while, open the fridge and wipe it up with a soapy rag a little bit and then close it again. I was angry he hired my mother, and we had a fight. I told him, "No way!"

After we argued for a while my husband said, "I am paying your mother the money to clean whether you let her clean the fridge or not!"

Seeing he had already paid my mother I decided to swallow my pride and let her clean it. She came over and started cleaning. I was amazed. She took every last thing out of the fridge; she threw away the old food. She washed all the shelves and then washed the ketchup bottles and jars and put everything back in. It looked wonderful. I learned how to clean a fridge that day. I had always just swished a washcloth around a little bit on the shelves around the food and called it done.   Ever since that day, I now clean the fridge the way I watched my mother do it. I had a lot to learn. I had to grow up, I couldn't open the fridge with my nose plugged and gag and then quickly close it anymore. It was my responsibility and I had to start cleaning it.

I learned that I had responsibilities now. I had to do them. I couldn't leave them for someone else. {There was no one else.} Not only was I supposed to be responsible for myself, but I was also now responsible for others too. It was hard work, but it had to be done.

What are We Leaving Behind?

Let's face it, we are only passing through this world. This is not our final resting place. What are we leaving behind? Do we leave messes behind us wherever we go? Messes that others have to deal with? Are we like the woman I mentioned who has left a wake of destruction behind her, trashing apartments and moving on leaving others with a huge mess and financial losses?

And there are more kinds of messes that leave others reeling, unseen messes but just as miserable. Divorces and broken marriages leave families in the rubble of emotional pain, children paying the price for the mess their parents leave them in. Some people cause pain wherever they go; they are like tornados leaving a trail of destruction on the people and places they go. And there are spiritual messes passed down on children and grandchildren from their forefathers who choose a life of sin.

To pass the test of life we want to leave the world behind us better than the way we find it. We don't want to leave a trail of garbage for others to deal with. When we move out of an apartment or a house, we have sold we want to leave it behind clean, in good repair and better than when we found it; with flowers growing in the yard.

We want to be a blessing to all those around us and those who go behind us, to those we know and love and to those we will never meet. We want to pick up our garbage and leave a clean path for those who are coming behind us. The sin stops with us. We want to be a channel of blessing to the world and bring life and healing to those we come across, in this life. We want to be givers and not takers. We want to repair the broken places, water the deserts, and make paths through the wildernesses that lead others to life.

We need to realize the trail behind us is evident to God, He sees what we fail to see ourselves. It is important to Him that we clean up our messes {Physical, financial, emotional and spiritual} so He can bless us and others!

Financial Garbage

I don't want to leave this world with a trail of financial garbage behind me. I don't want to leave bills unpaid. This has been difficult because of medical bills. I have had to have five surgeries in two years and my husband one. I have unpaid medical bills. This takes diligence. I am trying to find ways to live on less so I can work on my bills. Things like this are hard but it is important that we take care of our responsibilities.

There are many leaving a trail of garbage in the financial realm. Some out of selfishness, they spend, spend, spend. They don't care who they hurt. I remember years ago when I worked on a paper route. There was an older man that had a paper route; he was working day and night. I asked him why he was working so much; he was at an age he should have been retired. He told me he had spent his life building a successful business which he sold to retire. The people who were buying his business immediately filed for bankruptcy and never paid him, leaving him with a total loss after a lifetime of work. They legally took this man for everything. I felt sorry for the man, but I really feel sorry for those who took his business. They have failed the test of this life, choosing to take rather than to give.

I know this is hard. It is hard for all of us. Others become in debt through no fault of their own. They lose a job or become ill. Those with no family to fall back on can easily get into trouble. And some never have any chance to begin with, such as foster kids who turn eighteen and get turned out on their own with no one to help them. Some will never get ahead without some outside help! I know this is hard, {believe me I know}, but don't despair I believe if you will try to pay your debts God will help you!

Emotional Garbage

What are you leaving behind in the hearts of those you come in contact with? Are you spreading the love of God or passing along your frustration? Are you throwing garbage into people's lives? The garbage of impatience, judgment, unkindness, unforgiveness, unkind words, etc., etc., etc... I remember thinking for many years of my adult life, that if someone did wrong to you, you were supposed to yell at them. I thought that was normal behavior that was how I grew up. God had to tell me it was wrong.

I had loaned my mother my car one day because hers had broken down. I told her I needed it back by four. My husband Jim had an appointment.

He was finally getting some help for some emotional problems he was dealing with; he was seeing a counselor who was well known and expensive. Even though it was stretching our budget, getting him help was so important to me that I would have paid anything. I wanted my mom home by four so we could make the appointment because even if we missed it, we would still have to pay for it.

Well, at four my mom didn't show up and as the minutes of Jim's appointment went by, I got more frustrated and madder. I waited and waited, hoping we would at least get a few minutes in of his appointment. She had forgotten the appointment and went shopping after work. She pulled up and I was boiling, and I let her have it. I yelled at her.

I was the one who was going to get counseling this day, not Jim. After I yelled, God spoke to me. He was not angry, He just told me, "Even if someone else is wrong, you are not to yell at them, that is not okay."

I remember being shocked when God said that. I really thought I was supposed to respond that way. I am so glad He set me straight. We don't want to treat people that way. We don't want to pass on frustration. I learned that day that we don't have the right to yell at anyone. We can't throw emotional garbage at others!

Another time God had to deal with me for throwing emotional garbage at others. I had suppressed anger for many years and God helped me to start letting it out. The results were, I went around angry for a while, as the rage I had suppressed was being released. But God did not want me to pass that rage onto others!

Well, one day I did. I was driving and came up to a left turn light. As I started to turn left the car on my right turned left also, I thought she was cutting me off. I laid on my horn in absolute anger. I did not just blow it. I felt such rage I kept my hand on the horn all through the turn. I saw the confused look on the woman's face as she took the brunt of my anger. She couldn't figure out what she did wrong.

I found out later the next time I came to that

intersection that they had changed the lanes; they had added an extra left turn lane to that corner, and she had been correct, and I was the one who was wrong. I felt so ashamed. God let me know that what I did was not okay in a subtle way. That was the last time my horn in that car ever worked. The next time I tried to beep at someone I found out my horn no longer worked. It was a good thing too, because I was angry for several months and I kept pounding on a horn that wouldn't beep. God had to stop me from throwing out emotional garbage with my car horn.

No Spiritual Garbage

What we do in the realm of the spirit has even more impact. We can affect many for good or bad, so let's make it for good. There are some in the past who lived in such a way that we are still feeling the effects. How about Adam? Our great great granddaddy, his fall in the Garden of Eden has affected each human being since. Sin gets passed down. It causes all kinds of problems for generations to come. We can leave a trail of spiritual garbage, or we can leave blessings. The way we live will spiritually affect our children and grandchildren for generations to come. Have you ever noticed preachers run in families? Those who truly live for God seem to raise up preachers.

Your New Family

We cannot help what family we are born into. We may inherit a ton of garbage passed down to us. But there is something I want you to know. When you come to Christ you inherit a new family, a family that has passed down blessings instead of curses. They have lived their lives for others.

You get a new Grandpa, Father Abraham, he is the father of those who live by faith. You can inherit his blessings. In fact, it brings him joy when you do. And there is more, we have a big family, there is King David, and he will teach you to worship. Jonah, he will teach you to obey, Job will teach you the beauty of suffering and Joseph will teach you to pass tests. Oh, that is just the beginning of this wonderful new family of yours; John will teach you all about love and Noah about saving your family through obedience, Moses about stepping out when God tells you to move, and your own Red Sea will part, and Paul about our new covenant. And there is so much more!! Daniel will teach you to follow God in the midst of unbelievers and Joshua to face your battles with courage.

You see these have lived their lives in such a way that they have paved the way before us to live in righteousness. They have erected pillars of faith along the road for us to follow and they are our eternal family. You can claim them as your own and they are more than willing to claim you as their own. You can do what they did, follow Christ and walk your own walk so faithfully that you also will light the path for those who will come behind you!

We are the followers of Christ. We are to restore, heal and redeem, just as He did. We are to leave this world better than the way we found it. We are not to leave garbage behind us; we are called to be a blessing.

Chapter Eighteen

Be Kind to Strangers

Don't forget to entertain strangers, for by so doing some have unwittingly entertained angels. Hebrews 13:2

It is important how we treat total strangers. Like the person who cuts you off in traffic, or gets your order wrong at the restaurant, or just their looks offend you, their pants aren't pulled up and their underwear show{teen-agers}. We don't want to be unkind to strangers, not only because God loves them but for other reasons as well. You never know when you are going to run into this person again. They may become your new supervisor or client at work or join your church or move next door, or they may become your new stepmother! {I am writing from experience!}

I read a true story one time about a man who needed a job. He had an interview for a job lined up and was hoping he would get hired. On the way to the interview there was a terrible rainstorm. The man saw a woman ahead with a flat tire. He knew if he stopped to help, not only would he be late for his job interview he would also be all wet. He stopped anyway and then went on to the interview. When he got onto the interview, to his surprise, there was the woman whose tire he had changed. She hired him on the spot!

You never know how something you do can affect someone else or start a reaction that affects many people. A smile or act of kindness to a complete stranger, maybe they are at the end of their rope and considering suicide, maybe a spouse just passed away or maybe they have never known love. Treat everyone just the way you would want to be treated. Treat them like you would treat your own loved one.

I read another inspiring story along these same lines. It was written by a police officer. The officer received an emergency call that a child was choking. He put on his signal and started racing toward the address. To his horror he found he could not get through because of some road construction. He stopped his car to try to figure out how to proceed when a construction worker on an earth mover hollered to him, "What is the matter!"

"Child choking!' the police officer called back.

"Follow me," the man on the earth mover called back, "I will make you a road."

The police officer followed as the earth mover made him a path. He was able to get through and he sped on to the address where the child was choking. As he ran into the house the hysterical mother handed the officer a little boy who had turned blue. He couldn't breathe. He quickly began working on the boy, turning him over and slapping his back. Out popped a button and the child began to breathe again. The police officer returned the now breathing child to his grateful mother.

The next day the police officer went back to thank the construction worker whose quick thinking had allowed him to save a child's life. He found the man and began to thank him. The man immediately began to cry.

"Don't cry," the police officer told him, "The child is fine. Thanks to you I got there on time, and I was able to save him."

"I know," the man said crying even harder, "that was my son."

How we treat strangers is important!!!!

Chapter Nineteen

Wrestling with God

Then Jacob was left alone; and a Man wrested with him until the breaking of the day. Now when He saw that He did not prevail against him, He touched the socket of Jacob's hip; and the socket of Jacob's hip was out of joint as He wrestled with him. And He said, "Let Me go for the day breaks." But he said, "I will not let you go unless You bless me!" So, He said to him, "What is your name?" He said, "Jacob." And He said, "Your name shall no longer be called Jacob, but Israel; for you have struggled with God and with man and have prevailed." Genesis 32: 24- 28

    Jacob's name means grabber. Jacob was born a twin; his brother Esau was born first and then Jacob was born grabbing his brother's heel. Jacob entered this world struggling and grabbing.

    Jacob had a great destiny in God. He would be instrumental in the forming of Israel, the people of God. But Jacob had some changes to make. Jacob left some enemies along his path and the first was his twin brother

Esau.

First, Jacob cunningly tricked his twin brother Esau out of his birth right. Then Jacob, with help from his mother tricks Esau out of his father's blessing. Esau was angry and planning to kill his brother Jacob, so Jacob, with help again from his mother, fled to her brother Laban, Jacob's uncle.

On the way Jacob has an encounter with God. He fell asleep and dreamed of a ladder between earth and heaven. He saw the angels going back and forth on the ladder. Then God appeared at the top and spoke to Jacob. God makes a covenant with Jacob and promises to be with him and bring him back to this land and give it to his descendants.

The dreamed scared Jacob, but he got up and anointed the place and called it Bethel, which means house of God. Then Jacob comes to his uncle Laban. Jacob ends up marrying Laban's two daughters and working for him for twenty years. Jacob is cunning with Laban also and ends up owning the best of his flocks. Laban's attitude toward Jacob changes and once again Jacob flees. This time he heads back home to his parents. Esau hears he is coming, and Jacob is scared. The last time Jacob saw his brother he had wanted to kill him.

Jacob has come full circle in his life. He grabbed from his brother the birthright and the blessing, and then he struggled with his father-in-law, over wages and came out with the best herd of sheep. He has made enemies wherever he went, and he has got himself up against the wall. He can't go back, his father-in-law has chased him down and might have fought him, but God warned Laban not to harm him. He has burned his bridges behind him, and he has burned his bridges before him. Jacob has come to the end of himself. He has nowhere else to go.

Coming to the End of Ourselves

We like Jacob, have a covenant with God but we still use all our efforts to try to grab out of life what we want, or even what we think God wants for us. The problem is as long as we are using our own strength, ability, schemes or plan we will always end up running around in circles. Like Jacob our own way will probably end up hurting others.

The time will come for us like Jacob when we can't go any further. The way will keep getting harder and harder until our ability is just used up. We are up against a wall. In Jacobs's case he wrestled with an angel. He wrestled for God's blessing. He refused to let go until he got it. He wanted God's way and no longer his own. So great was his struggle and so deep was the change that God even changed Jacob's name to Israel. He went from Jacob which means grabber, or even wrestler, to Israel which means Prince. His name change reflected his inner change. He also walks with a limp now. The angel has touched his hip and put it out of place. Jacob can no longer depend on his own strength.

Jacob was a new man. He now sees that he is not in control God is. The next day he comes face to face with Esau. Things have changed overnight. They embrace and for the first time in their lives there is brotherly love between them. It took a struggle, a huge struggle but it is done, Jacob is never the same again.

Wrestling with God

We need to realize that if we wrestle with God, we will never out power Him. If we hang onto God and refuse to let go, like Jacob, God will bless us. In order for us to continue to hang on hard enough to press in for God's blessing we will no longer be able to hold onto our own devices. The struggle is just too intense. We will have to let go of our selfishness and our pride, if we hang onto those, we will lose our hold on God. We will have to let go of our own insecurities and motives and plans, we will have to let go of everything to wrestle with God and prevail. The only stubbornness we can hold onto is to stubbornly hold onto God. But if we prevail throughout the night, wrestling until morning, until the light comes, He will bless us and give us a new name that reflects the change in us. We will also see a change in our circumstances because God is now in control.

Intense Struggle

Our struggle with God is not quite so obvious as Jacob's but every bit as real. Our flesh, our old man, our sinful nature struggles to maintain control in our lives. The moment we become born again our spirit man is now united with God through the Holy Spirit, but our soul is a different story. We have a consistent struggle with our soul bringing it into submission to the Holy Spirit.

This is how we daily take up our cross and follow Christ, by daily crucifying the flesh, the old sinful thoughts and desires of the old sinful nature. We read about this in the Bible, *For the weapons of our warfare are not carnal but mighty in God for pulling down strongholds, casting down arguments and every high thing that exalts itself against the knowledge of God, bringing every thought into captivity to the obedience of Christ, and being ready to punish all disobedience when your obedience is fulfilled. 2 Corinthians 10:5-6*

You will notice in this verse we are having to war, and this war has to do with bringing thoughts in obedience to Christ. The struggle is a struggle of becoming obedient, obeying God and no longer our sinful flesh. This is the struggle, the intense struggle.

Summer's Intense Struggle

I can surely relate to intense struggle with my selfish disobedient flesh. Every woman who has become a mother can. Maybe my struggle was a little worse because I was extremely self- centered before I had children. I was like a big ME hole. Lots of times I didn't even eat, I was too lazy to even make myself something to eat. {I wish I had that problem now.}

Along comes three children of my own and two more to watch, my two baby sisters. The thing about kids is they are 24 hours a day seven days a week. My life was no longer a Me hole, it was all about kids, kids, kids. I did not want to get up in the middle of the night to feed a baby and change diapers, I wanted to sleep! I did not want to constantly hold a crying kid. I wanted to scream.

Believe me, I wrestled. I would wrestle myself. My kids would be crying and wanting me to pick them up and I wanted to scream and run. Sometimes I would lock myself in the bathroom or leave the kids in the house and drive around the block until I could win the wrestling match and be a loving mother again. I would think, "I can't do this anymore."

And then I would tell myself, "It doesn't matter what you think you can't do, you have to do what your children need. God gave you these children, this is your responsibility. They need you, now."

That would help. I would die to the big ME again and pick up my crying child and love them.

{Do you see why I was so amazed at the story in chapter 16 about the Pastor and the baby box and the handicapped children he so lovingly and patiently cares for day after day! I had such a struggle caring for my own not just someone else's. I had intense struggle with my ugly selfish self!}

The Angel Shama

In her wonderful book, *The Heavens Opened,* Anna Rountree, the author, tells us of an angel named Shama she meets in heaven. She describes him, he had long silver hair and he was very muscular. He is wearing a long white robe that looks like it has been stained either by blood or grape juice. The stain is on the hem and cuffs of his robes, from his elbows down and from his knees down. I will quote Anna's conversation with Shama.

"You delight in God," he continued. "I have watched you and have seen that you desire nearness to Him. However, do you not know that disobedience creates a wall between you and Him? It is a wall of your own making because you cannot curb your natural desires. He will replace with Himself every delight you push away, Anna." In looking at me, his eyes caught sight of a hill slightly beyond us. "Come with me," he said.

As we walked up the hill, he continued, "There is a type of suffering in obedience, but the rewards far, far outweigh the pain"

"Why is your robe stained at the bottom and on the sleeves?"

"I am called to assist in child training—the kind that squeezes the child—like being in a wine press. These," he said looking down at the stains, "are visible signs of the child's development. The more stains, the greater work has progressed within the child. Obedience is not learned easily Anna. Some on earth never learn it."

"Are you an angel assigned to help train me?" I asked. "I am assigned to you."

"Helping to train people in obedience cannot be a pleasant job."

The angel replied, "It is of great significance to the Father and absolutely necessary. By this time in your life, my robe should be entirely stained and my face and hands dripping, but there are only stains on the hem and sleeves. So, may I suggest that you are hindering your growth by disobedience. Immediate gratification can never replace serving the Lord with a whole heart. Such obedience releases joys untold."

Later in the conversation Anna thanks Shama.

I thank you for your patience and for helping me. I can see you are a powerful angel. If you were a human, I would say you 'worked out.'"

"We do, 'work out,'" he laughed heartily, "But our workout comes from wrestling with humans. I look as I do because you have given me so much resistance through your flesh. So," he laughed, "you might say I do 'work out'. I would suggest that you turn this very day so that my work out is less strenuous. Delight yourself in God. Anna and reduce my exercise program," he smiled.

It seems wrestling with angels wasn't just for Jacob. No wonder our lives aren't easy there is a struggle going on, a struggle that has high priority with God. A struggle like Jacob had, to come to the end of grabbing from others and doing things our own way. A struggle to accept God's will for us and to stop serving the big ME. The struggle may leave us with a limp so that we will realize that we do not live by our own strength or by our own schemes and devices but now we live by obedience to God. It is a huge change; we go from grabbers to a Prince of God. The change is evident. The struggle is intense, but it is well worth the reward.

In the words of the angel Shama, "Obedience releases joys untold."

Chapter Twenty

Take Heed

Therefore, let him who thinks he stands take heed lest he fall. 1Corinthians 10:12

We can never get to the point in our life where we think we have arrived and are incapable of falling. We cannot become careless. We are saved by grace. It is by grace we stand in the kingdom of God and not by our own works. We are standing in the middle of the path of life by the grace of God, but too often we fall onto one side or the other. On one side we take our eyes off of the Lord and onto ourselves. We feel unworthy and sinful, and we see ourselves as useless. We wonder how God could ever use us and we fall. We feel too unworthy or broken to be used by God.

On the other side we see what God has done through us and we think we are really something now. We think because God has done something through us that we know all about God and we are right and everyone else is wrong and God won't do anything apart from us. We become critical of anyone who believes differently than us.

And we fall on the other side. I have done both. Both of these are the result of self-centeredness.

Self-centeredness will always cause us to fall; it is a form of pride. This is how Lucifer fell. He beheld the glory of God, but he began to look to himself rather than God and he took pride in his position and power. Satan's sin was pride, and it caused his fall. Satan has set up a kingdom to himself. A kingdom that operates apart from God, a prideful and evil kingdom dedicated to himself.

Pride will cause us to build a life for ourselves apart from God, a kingdom of selfishness where we sit on the throne and serve ourselves. Most of us do this anyway. We give God a little portion of our lives and we give Him a little of our time and a little of our money, but it is really ourselves that we are serving.

Jesus told us to seek first the kingdom of God and his righteousness, and all these things would be added unto us. We want to follow Jesus' example not Satan's. Jesus teaches the opposite of pride, and that is humility.

Humility does not set up a kingdom to ourselves. The person with the attitude of humility realizes that we stand in the righteousness of Christ Jesus. He has bought us with a price, and we are in right standing with God. Humility agrees with the truth. We are righteous through the blood of Jesus. But we are not righteous apart from Him; we were created to be in Him, and this is the only way to become all we are meant to be and to truly be fulfilled. Our works are done by operating in obedience to Him and to bring Him glory and to build His kingdom.

Do Not Follow Men

Many Christians fall because they get disappointed in other Christians, a leader or a pastor, someone they followed and admire. There have been leaders of huge ministries that have fallen and those who followed them closely were hurt and became discouraged. Our goal should not be to be like our favorite minister or Christian leader but to be like the Lord. This will keep us steady when we find out our leaders are human. We can be like Jesus. Following Jesus closely and not men, is what will keep us from falling in this way.

Falling Christians

When Christians fall it can mean many things. Some may completely lose their faith and walk away from God permanently or for a time. We can through prayer take back captives from the enemy. Remember the Bible says we can repent for another person as long as it is not a sin unto death. *If anyone sees his brother sinning a sin which does not lead to death, he will ask, and He will give him life for those who commit sin not leading to death. I do not say that he should pray about that. All unrighteousness is sin, and there is sin not leading to death. 1John 5:16-17*

We say spiritual warfare for a reason, we are in a war with the enemy and the spoils are souls! When we see a brother or sister in the Lord who has fallen, we need to pray for them and fight for them.

Falling can also mean that a Christian gets taken captive by the enemy in some area of their life, it can be deception or lust or some sin, it could be sickness or a strong delusion, or even mental illness. Think of it literally as a real war, which it is, and some of ours get captured. They are held hostage by the demonic forces. You may still see them, but something has changed. They can no longer get free in a certain area of their life. They may also be used by the enemy to fight other Christians.

Rick Joyner in his book, *The Final Quest*, saw a huge demonic army and they were riding on the backs of Christians. Some of the divisions he saw were Pride, Self-Righteousness, Respectability, Selfish Ambition, Unrighteous Judgement, and Jealousy. They carried weapons of slander, intimidation, accusation, gossip and faultfinding. These did not even realize they were being used by the enemy in his army and his attack on the church. They thought they were being used by God, and although these people from all walks of life professed Christianity, they were living their lives in agreement with the enemy. The enemy was using this demonic army that was riding on the Christians to attack the church. The enemy worked by deception.

To be honest with you, all of those things Rick saw in that army I have done.

Don't Agree with Your Enemies

I have noticed something from being around a lot of recovering alcoholics for so many years. Their enemy also works by deception. We learn in the AA world about a thing called denial. Denial is what keeps alcoholics drinking. Denial gets the alcoholic to agree with his enemy. The stronghold of alcoholism tells the alcoholic, you don't have a problem everyone else does. This evil gremlin convinces the alcoholic to keep taking one more drink, and one more drink and one more drink. It gets the alcoholic to blame everyone else for their problems, but they never blame the alcohol, that is their best friend.

Something really wonderful happens when an alcoholic starts getting better. They stop agreeing with their enemy. They come out of agreement with the denial. That is when they get free. I have seen it happen to people and it is a wonderful thing. Alcoholics that are mothers suddenly stop thinking about alcohol and start thinking about their children again. Fathers start thinking about their children again and husbands about their wives and children about their parents.

The alcohol had set them against everyone while they agreed with it, it sucked the life out of them, and they became so different they were hardly recognizable. As they agreed with their enemy they were formed into a different person. By agreeing with their enemy, they were transformed into its image. Alcohol came first, even before those they loved.

It is the same for all of us, with all our enemies, we have to stop agreeing with them. Bitterness wants us to never forget what others have done. He reminds us of how others have hurt us over and over. Gluttony always tells us we are going to die of something, why not be happy and eat whatever we want, whenever we want. And no matter how much we eat it is never enough.Selfishness tells us we have to get all we can and forget about the other guy; no one else is going to think about us. Selfishness will even cause a mother to kill her own child in her womb, so she won't be tied down.

Lust turns others into objects that gratify our selfish pleasures, to the lustful, other people really do not count. Laziness always gives us an excuse not to do something. Adultery says this is no big deal and your wife doesn't understand you, as you pick another fight with her so you can blame her while you go spend time with someone you shouldn't. While gambling tells you, you will never win if you don't play, and you never do win because you never can win enough.

The moment we fall out of agreement with our enemies and into agreement with the truth we become free. Our enemy has three objectives in our life, to steal to kill and to destroy. The more we agree with him the more he works his sinister objectives. So, why should we agree with him?

Grace and Mercy

The important thing to remember is this, when we fall to get back up. Satan has never won a battle if you are still fighting. If you are still trying it is not over yet. Humility and repentance will get you back on track. God will forgive us and restore us.

Sometimes that process of restoration can take a while. I have had two major falls in my Christian walk. Both times it took me years to feel like I had gotten back to where I had been before.

There are a few things I feel that will guard us from falling and they are the Word of God, following the voice of the Holy Spirit, and walking in humility.

Remember, to be careful, the Bible tells us to take heed. The enemy works by deception, we have to come out of agreement with him. No matter how many times we have fallen, if we keep getting up, we haven't lost yet. And God will forgive you when you ask; He will pick you up and restore you.   *Rejoice not against me, Oh my enemy; When I fall, I shall arise, when I sit in darkness, the Lord shall be my light. Micah7:8*

Chapter Twenty-One

The Rest Test

There remains therefore a rest for the people of God. For he who has entered His rest has himself ceased from his works as God did from His. Hebrews 4:9-10

Entering God's rest is a key to our salvation, but it is also a key to passing the tests of life. There is a place we can come to in the midst of our own trials, struggles and turmoil where we let go of the outcome we desire and begin to let God do whatever He wants, and we enter His rest. It has happened to me in areas of my life. It has also happened to others in areas of their life. And to some like the apostle Paul it has happened to his entire life. This is what we need. It is an awesome experience that enables you to go through unbelievable circumstances with perfect peace because you have entered His rest.

A Prison Inmate Enters Rest

My husband Jim experienced this rest in prison.

Being locked up was nothing new to my husband Jim. He seemed to be born into trouble. He had been locked up as a child; kept by his mother locked up alone in the closet while his siblings were allowed their freedom. Then in his early teens he spent much time in juvenile homes, jails for kids. Being locked up was becoming a way of life for him. It continued on to the county jail as he grew older and then the house of correction.

Even though he had become a Christian he had a long way to go. He had never known love or anything normal and his life still spiraled downward. He was also not new to violence having been beaten as a child, not to mention stabbed, shot, knocked unconscious and hit by a car.

He was also used to having enemies, having been involved in the Mafia and he left on not so good terms. He also had a one-man war with a motorcycle gang who had raped someone he cared about. Also surviving all his incarcerations taught him violence as a way of life. But even after all this he was not ready for prison. By his early twenties he was given a prison sentence of three to fifteen years.

Entering prison was terrifying and Jim's worst fears were confirmed. Jim was sentenced to Jackson Prison, the largest walled maximum-security prison, a sinister place. As frequently happens to new inmates to the system, a gang of hardened homosexual men vowed to get Jim. They surrounded his cell, breathing threats and vowing to get him and reaching through the bars. Jim attacked back throwing hot water in their faces and anything he could find to throw at them.

Jim was put into solitary confinement for his own protection and then later transferred to minimum security. Jim used the chance to escape, and he headed for Colorado.

In Colorado, where Jim managed to stay for nine months before getting caught, he connected with Christians and began to grow spiritually. After nine months he was pulled over for a burned-out taillight and apprehended. Then Jim was placed in the county jail in Colorado waiting to be sent back to Michigan. Jim's stay in the county jail stretched into several months. There he led his cell mate to the Lord, and they continued to read their Bibles and pray together. As the time stretched on Jim began to have hope that he would not be extradited back to Michigan.

Michigan had ninety days to retrieve Jim and if they didn't come in that time frame he would be let go. As the days went by Jim began to think maybe the Lord would deliver him from his prison sentence and his worst fears of going back to the hell hole he had escaped from. Then on the very last day before he would be let go the authorities from Michigan arrived and Jim was once again on his way to face one of the worst maximum-security facilities in the country.

But something was different this time. Jim knew he couldn't do this on his own, so he turned himself over to God. He let go and somehow, he discovered God's rest. He was by no means perfect, but he was at peace for the first time in his life. He was facing the thing he feared the worst, but something was different he had ceased striving; he felt a peace he knew he was in God's hands.

It still was not pleasant it was hell on earth, but Jim walked through the midst of hell with God. Jim saw stabbings and killings. One time a young man overcome the horrors of prison, jumped off the fourth floor of the cell block to his death below, Jim witnessed this, but he was experiencing a rest and a supernatural protection.

Because of his escape Jim spent the next four years in maximum security. He was with serial killers and hardened men. At one point the warden received a tip there was a contract put out on Jim's life and he was again put in solitary confinement. But Jim was already in a safe place because he had entered God's rest. It was still awful, but his heart was at rest.

When I met Jim, after he had gotten out of prison, he was no longer at rest. He didn't know how to survive on the outside and was not doing well. He would talk of his time in prison and feeling so close to God. Back then I did not know what he was talking about. It sounded to me sometimes like he wanted to go back. I was confused and asked him, "Do you want to be back in prison?"

"No," he said realizing how awful that would be, "I just want to be that close to the Lord again."

Summer Enters God's Rest

I have since learned about entering God's rest having experienced it for myself several times. One particular time had to do with my son, Jamie. As soon as Jamie was born, I got into my head I never wanted him to go through what his dad went through. I never wanted him to go to jail or prison. It was kind of an inner vow I made to myself; I had to make sure this didn't happen.

When he was a little kid, I would drag him up to the front and have him prayed over. "His dad has spent many years in jails and prison," I would tell the ministers, "I don't ever want that for my son." They would look down at my sweet little boy and then look at me like I was a nut; but they would pray. I just wanted to be sure, so I got prayer about it.

Well, as it turned out Jamie had serious learning disabilities just like his dad did. School became torture for him because he couldn't do the work. Every year the school would pass him because of his size {big!} But every year he got further behind. Jamie would get bored while all the kids did their work, and he was lost. He started acting up. In third grade, he locked his whole class including the teacher in the closet where the cubbies were kept. His behavior at school continued to get worse.

I used all my effort to try to fix things. We would do homework for hours after school trying to catch him up. While his sisters were playing, he would be trying to do his schoolwork all night long. His learning disabilities were severe. One summer break I had him do school studies all summer long. When school started, he seemed caught up but as soon as a couple weeks passed back at school he was lost again. I even took him out of school for one year and worked with him all day. Jamie felt cut off from his friends and wondered why he was different.

By the time he was in Junior High he was sitting there all day unable to do the work the rest of the class was doing. He was doing nothing. He started to vent his frustration by getting in fights at school. All of a sudden, my sweet little boy was getting in trouble all the time.

One time the school called the police, and they took Jamie away in hand cuffs. My horrible fears were being realized and I was angry and fearful, mostly fearful. I was falling apart at the seams. I had to keep him out of jail! I was fighting on both sides. I was constantly punishing Jamie, trying to straighten him up. I was fighting for Jamie with the schools. I was using all my effort and things just kept getting worse. Why wasn't God helping me more? Why was this world such a cold, hard cruel place that I couldn't get my son the help he needed!

We went to court, and I was weak from fear. I had to fight to keep from fainting. I felt like someone who had the wind knocked out of them. This is the one place I never ever wanted to be with my son and here I was. As we stood before the judge I wondered if anyone could possibly know how I felt. All the times I had been in this position with my husband, this was worse. This was my son. Thank goodness he got probation.

I hounded the school to help him learn so they took him out of school and put him in another school for the kids having trouble. It was supposed to be a career tech. but what it was, was a nightmare. It was a school full of drugs and violence. Things got worse. Jamie, always the entrepreneur, rolled up a piece of wax and tried to sell it as a rock, {some kind of drug}. The school police officer called me and was he mad. He saw Jamie trying to sell this supposed rock and chased him, but Jamie was too fast. The officer sprained his ankle chasing him. It turns out selling a little piece of wax was as bad as selling the real thing, or so he told me.

I begged and pleaded for mercy. This was so traumatic for me I was walking around like the living dead; in fact, I would have rather been dead. I was falling apart. Things continued to go wrong; next Jamie got into a little tussle at the church youth group. Even though the other boy started it Jamie got into trouble because he was bigger. The other boy's mother wanted the police involved and was making a big fuss. I hoped she would change her mind. I asked the pastor talk to her, and he did, but even he couldn't change her mind.

This woman had been in trouble with law a couple of years before and was facing prison and the judge had mercy on her and gave her no sentence. It was a a miracle that she often told people about, so I thought she would have mercy, but she refused. I felt such anger toward this woman; couldn't she see the hell she was putting me through?

I prayed, I cried, I wailed. God heard from me every minute of the day. I felt like the world had come to an end. We had to go to court again. It turned out okay, the judge was merciful, Jamie just continued on probation. Things settled down. But the joy went out of living for me that was just too close of a call. I took Jamie out of school and began teaching him at home, that helped him stay out of trouble.

A couple of years later we moved to Michigan. Jamie was now sixteen. I could not teach him at home anymore because I had to work full time during the day. He was on his own about education. He enrolled in a program for students who were behind trying to graduate. Soon all his friends again were troublemakers. I tried to talk to Jamie who was going the wrong direction again. He told me, "Mom, I just don't care what happens to me. The only thing that bothers me is that I am hurting you."

Jamie had given up on himself. I just didn't know what to do. I was so tired of struggling and living with the fear of Jamie getting into trouble and going to jail. I came to the end of myself. I just couldn't go on like this. I loved my son so much, but all my striving and worrying and doing everything I knew to do was futile. I had run into a brick wall and there was nowhere else to go. I went to God.

"Lord," I prayed, "I give Jamie back to You. Even if letting go of him means jail. I am letting go, Jamie is in Your hands now."

I had just let go of my biggest fear. I had just decided whatever happened to my son that God was in control. I had freed myself from that inner vow I had made when my son was born, that I had to keep from jail at all costs. I had just stopped striving and I had just entered God's rest. It was His struggle now. For the first time in a long time, I felt peace. I took a deep breath, it felt so good. I could breathe again; that tight, sickening, strangling, fear that had consumed me was gone.

Jamie was friends with a new boy he had met at

school named Jack. Jack was a really bad character. He lived with his dad, but his dad was seldom home. I was not in control anymore; God was in control, but I felt He wanted me to have a talk with Jamie about Jack. I sat Jamie down and we read a devotional together. It was written by a young man who was a Christian but got in the wrong crowd and he succumbed to peer pressure and the lesson he learned. Jamie listened intently but he told me he knew he could handle things. I knew it was God's word to Jamie.

"Aw, Mom," Jamie said, "Jack is a good guy, you just don't know him like I do."

Jamie went to Jack's house that night, but he didn't come home the next day as planned. In fact, we didn't know where he was until we got a call from the police department the next day. Jamie was in jail! He had been arrested for under aged drinking.

Something was drastically different this time. I was at peace. I wasn't happy but I was at peace. It was no longer my problem; I had let go. I was at rest; no more striving.

You need to realize if this had happened before I probably would have had a nervous breakdown at this point. I literally could not have dealt with this. I was shocked at how peaceful I felt. It felt so much better than the fear and the torment I had been going through for years.

I went down to the police station in a bubble of God's presence. I was calm and relaxed talking to the police and not begging as I would have been. The officer told me that Jamie and the boys he had been with were picked up by the arresting officer in a car and all the boys had been drinking. He also said the boys had stolen a stereo system and some C.D.'s out of another car the night before.

Jamie had cooperated with the detective and had been truthful, he told the police everything. Jamie hadn't had anything to do with stealing, but he had helped the boys move the stuff later. When the police officer told me how Jamie had cooperated with him, I felt relieved, that sounded more like how I raised my son. The other boys lied but Jamie told them where to find the stereo and everything was recovered except for several C.D.'s.

I was rational and not hysterical which was new for me, so I had the presence of mind to ask the officer, "If the boys were stealing, why are you letting them go?"

I felt like I took the officer off guard with my attitude so he confided in me, "All three boys will be charged with felonies, including your son. We will charge him with receiving stolen property because he didn't steal it, but he helped the other boys move it later. Because he is seventeen, we will be charging him as an adult."

I sucked in my breath; I was hearing the unbelievable, my son, my own beloved son was facing prison time. It was the worst thing, in my mind, that could ever happen to me, {and my son}. It was the one thing I told myself could never happen and it was happening. Yet the most amazing thing to me was that I knew God was in control. I was staying out of control and leaving God in control. Not that it was pleasant, but, yet it was, it was pleasant to let go and be at peace on the worst day of my life.

It was like being in a tornado, you could hear the wind blowing, you can feel the house shaking, but you're in the basement, you're in a shelter, the storm is there but you are protected. The most important thing in my whole world, my son's life was being shaken, but I had given my son's life back to God. It was no longer mine to protect.

On the way home I told my son what the officer had told me. He got very quiet. When we got home, he hung his head and retreated to his room. The next day he approached me, "Mom," he said, "Remember when I told you I didn't care what happens to me?" I nodded. "Well, I do care, "he added.

I knew he had been doing some soul searching. "Will you drive me to church?" {His dad and I had not allowed him to get a driver's license because he had been getting into trouble.}

I was more than happy to drive Jamie to church. A nearby church was having a youth group and he asked to be dropped off there.

I no sooner got home when the phone rang, it was Jamie, he asked me to come get him. "I am sorry, mom," Jamie said as he got back in the car, "But these kids aren't serious about the Lord. Can you drop me off at the Assemblies of God Church?"

Jamie found what he was looking for at the next church, a group of young people that were sold out for the Lord. Jamie recommitted his life to the Lord that night.

Suddenly Jamie was voraciously seeking the Lord.

One church was not enough for him. He was going to three. Every night he went somewhere to pray, worship or help out. He volunteered to teach at Vacation Bible School. He also went to several youth meetings per week. He was not the same kid. He was on fire for the Lord.

Soon not just Jamie had recommitted his life to the Lord but his younger sister and cousin too, they wanted in on what Jamie had. It affected Jim and I too. Because of moving to a new town and our new work schedules my husband and I hadn't been going to a church yet, but we followed Jamie to one of his new churches.

Jamie's zeal was having an effect on everyone. He was so busy I never quite knew what he was up to or what he was doing. My sister told me how at one church Jamie was helping in the children's church. One little boy was a terrible problem, and the teachers couldn't control him until Jamie started helping. Jamie had a special way with him, and he sat on Jamie's lap all through class. Everyone was amazed at the change in the little boy.

I heard more. I was at work one day and a woman I worked with told me, "You can't believe how much your son has helped a friend of mine. Her husband left and her ten-year-old son was filled with rage until your son started spending time with him. The change in her son is unbelievable." I had remembered Jamie toting a little guy around with him.

I had to pinch myself. My son's life had dramatically changed. Jamie had really changed. God had done more in my son's life than I could have possibly dreamed. You see the most important thing for me, in my life was and still is, is that I want my children to serve the Lord, not just half-heartedly but whole-heartedly. My greatest desire was being fulfilled and not just for my son. His zeal had spread to his sisters as well and even given a boost to me and my husband. But we still had a court case looming. Jamie had decided to plead guilty.

Normally his court case in the future would be like a black shadow following me around and sucking the life out of me but this time it wasn't. I was still at rest. Jamie was a little nervous, but he also had put it in God's hands.

Jamie came home from his job at a fast-food place one night with a great big smile on his face. He had a story to tell me. He was feeling apprehensive about his court case, and he asked God to send him an angel to let him know everything was going to be okay. He had been reading a book on angels and he had asked God to send him one. After his prayer, he was waiting expectantly for God to send him an angel. At work that day, as he broke open a roll of pennies, the top penny rolled out and the penny had an angel carved out of the center of it. He gasped. It was a penny from heaven to him. He felt God was assuring him his prayer was answered. He carried that penny with him every day.

As the court day got nearer, we all wrote letters to the judge telling him how well Jamie was doing. When the day finally came, we were hoping for the best, but we were all disappointed. I don't think the judge bothered to read the letters or even find out what the case was about. Jamie hadn't done any stealing, he had just helped move the stolen equipment. He sentenced Jamie, six months to two years. I knew God was still in control. God was doing what was best.

The good news was Jamie was going to serve his time in the local county jail and he was going to get to keep going to school every day. Because of our work schedule neither my husband nor I could be there when he needed to be picked up, so his youth pastor and his wife transported him every day from jail to school.

Jail did not dampen Jamie in the least. He led his cellmate to the Lord, and they prayed together. He also led two other men to the Lord while he was there. After four months Jamie was able to come home on house arrest. When Jamie turned eighteen, he entered adult classes and got his GED. Then when he was off probation Jamie enrolled in Bible College.

When I stopped striving over my son's life and entered God's rest, God did beyond what I could have ever imagined. I had never dreamed Jamie would ever graduate high school let alone go to college because of his learning disabilities. College was difficult for him and took him an extra year but his senior year he made the dean's list.

I love this rest stuff. I need more of it. But there is even a higher level of rest, listen to this.

God is our refuge and strength, a very present help in trouble. Therefore, we will not fear, even though the earth be removed, And though the mountains be carried into the midst of the sea: Though its waters roar and be troubled, though the mountains shake with its swelling. Psalm 46:1-3

Can you imagine that level of peace and rest! Can

you imagine seeing the earth breaking up in front of you and yet you have no fear. Everything you know being moved and shaken and yet staying in peace in the peace and refuge of our God! That is the way I want to live! I want to tell you another story I read about a woman who entered this rest right in the midst of her worst fears and trouble ever. She called it the nevertheless principle.

The Nevertheless Principle

I read a wonderful book called the, *Nevertheless Principle*, by Marion Bond West. It is such a good book I have read it over and over. Marion writes about her struggle when she was faced with the worst thing imaginable to her, her husband, Jerry, was diagnosed with a malignant brain tumor.

Losing her husband of twenty-five years was unthinkable to her. She had grown up without a father, something that had been devastating to her, now the thought of losing her husband hit her with a blow that paralyzed her with fear. She prayed as well as getting everyone she knew to pray and for a short while her husband went into remission, but it didn't last.

Fighting her fear was such a battle that it took all her strength. Everything else in her life stopped. She desperately wanted to hang onto her husband and her life as she knew it, but it just kept slipping away.

Then something happens to her, when she comes to the end of herself, she finally finds peace. It started on her way home from the hospital one day; she had been driving back and forth from the hospital for several days when her miracle began.

She calls it nevertheless living. Driving home, she describes the sun's rays coming in the car and she gets a feeling she describes as golden, something like joy and peace. She had a premonition that something good was about to happen, but she didn't know what. She went to bed that night with a sense of expectation.   She found out the next morning as she was waking, early. As she was waking a question formed in her mind, she asked God, {I'll quote the book]

Father, where am I in my spiritual walk now? What's happening?

I could imagine God smiling and saying, *I'm glad you asked that.* **He seemed to go on to explain:** *You are at the crucial moment now. You have been shipwrecked and nearly drowned in the icy waters of fear. But you've kept swimming and you are in reach of an island. Right now, you can crawl up on the shore and be safe there.*

"Father what is the name of the island?"

It's called the Island of Trust. You will be alone on it but you will be safe. If you stay on it nothing will hurt you. **I imagined myself crawling up on the island. I was getting out of the cold choppy waters. The white sand on the island was warm like the clothes out of the dryer. I lay down on the sand. There were palm trees and a flag on the island. The flag was red with white letters that spelled "Trust." It flapped in the wind.**

Marion entered a real place although it seemed imaginary. It was so real it gave her peace through the things she was about to go through, the death of her husband. No longer was she in torment. In her conversation with God which continued, He warned her others, well-meaning people, would come and try to get her off the island. And He warned her not to listen, not to go out to them and not to even put her feet in the water because she would experience fear again if she were to leave the island of trust. On the island of trust, she relinquishes to God her husband Jerry. Then God tells her, *"Doesn't it feel good to have given up the struggle? It's all My struggle now. You could have done this long ago. But I understand you and how your mind and emotions have to struggle. Relinquishment is very hard. Many people find it impossible, so they never reach this wonderful island that I have prepared for My shipwrecked children.*

Marion has passed the rest test. Jerry passes away and Marion never leaves the island of trust. The thing she most fears happens, and she is at peace every minute through it. She has come to the point that she has relinquished to God her life and the expectations she had for her life. She has ceased struggling and entered God's rest. In the midst of her greatest trial in life she feels warm and safe. She is in a place of refuge. It is still hard, but it is so peaceful in God's rest.

Can We Live this Way?

Can we live this way????? Can we live our whole lives this way????? Can we face anything and stay at peace? Can we face the death of a loved one or even our own death and stay at peace? Can we face disaster of every kind and stay at peace? Can we even face the earth being removed and the mountains being cast into the sea? Can we face heart ache, danger, peril, financial problems, family problems, or even the things happening in our country and the world and be at peace???? Can we cease from all our struggling, our striving and our futile attempts to control our lives, our future and our loved ones and relinquish it to God and enter into His rest?

The time may come, who knows, that we may have to lay down our lives for the sake of the gospel. Persecution is coming and even in America. We can have peace in any situation that we relinquish to God. It doesn't mean it is pleasant, but as long as we stay on the island of trust, we are safe from fear.

I read a story one time of the persecuted Chinese Christians. A Christian Chinese man and his wife and children were told to renounce their faith or be killed by communist soldiers. They refused to renounce their faith. The soldiers dug a pit and put the whole family inside. As the little family huddled together in the pit the soldiers began to throw shovels full of dirt into the pit. The soldiers told the Christian family if you renounce your faith, we will pull you out of the pit.

The children, being shorter, began to suffocate first and their father longing to protect his children called out in defeat; he would say or do anything to protect his children. But his wife had peace, she stopped him, and she stopped the soldiers from pulling them out. She said, "No, we will stay," and she said to her children, "In just a few minutes we will all be together in Heaven!"

Her husband took heart, and they were able to sing and rejoice as the family was buried together. They were able be strong even watching their children suffer. Their rest carried them through to ultimate victory. They all entered Heaven together.

Can we relinquish our whole life? I believe Paul the apostle lived this way. He said in scripture, *I have been crucified with Christ; it is no longer I who live, but Christ lives in me; and the life which I now live in the flesh I live by faith in the Son of God, who loved and gave Himself for me. Galatians 2:20*

Chapter Twenty-Two

Passing the Test of the Times

And do not be conformed to this world, but be transformed by the renewing of your mind, Romans 12:2

When my two older kids Jamie and Lonna were four and two, they were between a rock and a hard place. We had just moved to Florida and to their delight they each had a new playmate. I was babysitting two little sisters who were also two and four and I became their new babysitter and they all had fun playing together. Their trouble came when their mother came home the two little sisters were allowed to play with all the kids next door and my kids weren't. It was an issue their mother and I disagreed on.

There was no way I would relent and allow my children to play with these children, not that it was the children's fault, but their parents were the most wicked people I had ever met. The reason I thought they were so wicked was because not only did they do drugs and sex, but they also did all this in front of their children and the oldest was six years old!

So, there were my kids every night watching all the other kids play and they were not allowed to join them.

There was no way I was going to expose my children to the things that were going on next door. My children felt left out and confused as all the other kids were playing and they watched from the window.

We stood alone. I refused to close my eyes to the things being done in front of small children and in a small way my not allowing my children around them was a nonverbal disapproval of their actions. I also spoke up and told their mother why my children weren't allowed to play. Soon the two little sisters that I babysat were describing gross sex acts in detail to their mother obviously from their association with these children.

Thank goodness we moved soon after and those times passed, they no longer felt left out, and the danger has passed. In a small way my children felt what many Christians have felt at various times throughout the ages. We can't agree with the things that go on and are being called normal, we are made to feel like we are intolerant, and we don't fit in with society. This is what my small children went through, they had to stand alone. My children had passed the test of the times.

Passing Times

I remember in junior high and high school, the test of the times was to "be cool". We lived in an area where there was a demonic stronghold of rebellion over the young people. To be cool meant to party, do drugs and you must never be seen with your parents, very uncool. It seemed like almost every kid in the school was into smoking, drinking and drugs. Certainly, the popular kids, it was the only way to be in the in crowd. The only kids that were able to stand the test of the times in that area were the "church kids" and those that had a very well-grounded relationship with their parents. It was normal to be bad.

To kids in junior high, friends and school seems like the whole world. It is hard to realize these times will pass. This mentality will pass. This is not truth just because it is the normal right here and now. And for some kids it didn't pass. Drugs are a destructive lifestyle; some kids died, either from car accidents in a car full of partying kids or overdoses.

I did not grow up in an area where gangs were a problem, but I know many kids do. To those kids in that situation the gang seems like the answer. To many it seems like the only way to get ahead. They get fast money from drugs and protection. But what we all see because we are not involved in the unreality that they are in, is that it is the fast track to destruction. And yet in the midst of these, there are kids who refuse to join the gangs, who often stand alone and take the hard way and make something of their lives. They pass the test of their times.

Whole societies get caught up into deception and follow cleverly crafted lies from the enemy, called popular thinking. Only those who are anchored in the unchanging truth of the Bible, the Word of God, are able to withstand the storms and raging seas of the constantly changing ideas and lies that shipwreck the rest of society. In these times Christians have to become beacons of light and stand for truth, many times standing alone, being mocked and scorned by those who are offended by truth. This is how they pass the test of the times. And these times do pass, and sanity is restored. Those who stood for truth are remembered as heroes, but new times come with different challenges.

In every age there have been tests of the times. In ancient times men married multiple wives, people worshipped idols and they offered their children as burned sacrifices to evil gods. These things are repulsive to us now. In more recent times we have had slavery which was even legal. It was considered normal by most. Those true Christians and others who opposed it had to break the law to help slaves to freedom. The horrors of slavery are repugnant to us now.

And what about the Nazi's during World War 2, who burned people in incinerators. Those who helped the Jewish people escape and were caught suffered the same fate and many died with them.

In our day we have just as many tests to face. We have to make a stand against them just as the true Christians have had to do all throughout history. Our issues have been abortion, sex sin, evolution, gay marriage, pornography and even a universal religion that removes Christ as our Savior and claims there are many ways to God. Why do we have to stand publicly for truth? It gets us mocked and punished, ridiculed and called narrow minded. Can't we just be neutral? I believe the answer to that is, No, even though it may cost us something.

During the test of the times when there is a

struggle between good and evil and between lies and the truth that never changes, it is important for you to make it clear where you stand. In some way you must be set apart from the thinking of the times. You must not be silent. There are several reasons for this. Number one, you are a witness to those who are caught up in deception. You will save some by speaking up for truth. Number two you separate yourself from the judgement that God sends on the lie, you are sealed from the judgement. Number three, you will bring courage to others who want to stand for truth. I am thinking of someone in the Bible who lived in a very wicked time among great wickedness, Lot.

Lot, in Sodom and Gomorrah

Lot lived in a time and place that the people in the city he was living were so evil that God destroyed his city and the nearby cities by raining fire down on them from heaven. We are told in *2Peter:6-8 And turning the cities of Sodom and Gomorrah into ashes, condemned them to destruction, making them an example to those who afterward would live ungodly; and delivered righteous Lot, who was oppressed by the filthy conduct of the wicked {for that righteous man, dwelling among them, tormented his righteous soul from day to day by seeing and hearing their lawless deeds}*

Lot was moved from the city before the destruction by angels. Lot lived a very different lifestyle in the midst of great evil. But one thing Lot failed to do was save anyone else except save himself and his two daughters.

I want to quote you a passage from Rick Joyner's book, *The Call,* in which Rick, in a prophetic vision has a conversation with Lot, which I found very interesting.

"I am Lot. You have been chosen to live in difficult times in which I was chosen. As Abraham lived and interceded for Sodom, you must do the same. During the time when great perversion is released on the earth, men and women of great faith will arise. Like Abraham, you must use your faith to intercede for the wicked, and you must also witness the judgement of God coming on the earth. The Lord cannot abide the increasing evil of mankind much longer. I was silent and many perished. You must not be like me—you must not be silent."

"Tell me more. How do I warn them?" I asked.

"I thought that I would be a warning just by being different. Being different is not enough! The power of the Holy Spirit to convict sin is released by the spoken word. What the Lord did to Sodom, He did as an example so that others would not have to be destroyed that way. You can warn those headed for destruction by telling them my story. There are now many cities whose evil He will not abide much longer. If those who know the Lord don't arise, there will be many more like Sodom very soon."

Lot later says, **"The people of earth are blind. They will not see if you simply try to be a witness. The message of judgement must go forth in words, but the words must be spoken in order for Him to anoint them."**

Standing up for truth must be lived and spoken.

Our goal is for mercy and for the salvation of those who are caught up in the current test of the times, and for truth to be restored, and it will be. We are called to bring life. Our two greatest weapons are truth and love. We are to speak the truth in love. We stand between light and darkness. We are the light shining into the darkness. Some will listen to the truth spoken in love and choose the light, others will see us and hear us and choose the darkness.

Some have given their lives to stand for truth.

The Truth about Homosexuality

The men in Sodom and Gomorrah were homosexuals that is where the word sodomy comes from. The Bible is very clear on the sin of homosexuality. Christians are being tested in this area because the current test of our times is to say that God made people this way. We don't get this from scripture; this is the current belief of our times. It used to be illegal in this country to commit sodomy. Now those Christians who stand up for the truth in this matter are coming under heavy criticism. It is becoming unpopular to stand up for the truth. This will only get worse. Recently our government took a stand on homosexual marriage directly opposing scripture.

What did the church do? Some opposed it, publicly. They passed this test of the times. Many decided to just accept it, caving under the pressure, afraid to stand for truth. It is no fun to be labeled intolerant or to be compared to racists, against human rights. {We as Christians are not against human rights, remember it was not those who followed the current times that stood up for human rights in the slave years, it was those who followed scripture, the unchangeable truth. Those who followed the thinking of those times were against human rights.} Remember the test of the times exchanges the truth for a lie.

It is getting harder and harder to stand up for truth, those who do so will become more and more criticized. The truth is becoming so offensive that those who speak out for it are considered intolerant and narrow minded.

Why Is It So Important?

Why is this current test so important? People say, "I know some homosexuals and they are very nice people." I agree. This is true. But we are not standing against people, we are standing against the lie that has them bound. God loves every sinner and that includes you and me, but the scripture has some very specific results if this sin is not repented of.

This current test is very important because it is a fore runner of a bigger test that is coming next. It is like a little quiz and the final exam is next. How you respond to this quiz may show you if you are ready for the exam that you and every person on this planet is about to take. This test that is coming will come about much as this issue did, this is a forerunner, and this will be the biggest test of the times, ever.

Chapter Twenty Three

Passing the Tests of the Times Part 2
"As It Was in the Days of Noah"

"And as it was in the days of Noah, so it will be in the days of the Son of Man: They ate, they drank, they married wives, they were given in marriage, until the day that Noah entered the ark, and the flood came and destroyed them all. Likewise, as it was also in the days of Lot; They ate, they drank, they bought, they sold they planted they built; but on that day that Lot went out of Sodom it rained fire and brimstone from heaven and destroyed them all. Even so it will be in the day when the Son of man is revealed. In that day, he who is on the housetop, and his goods are in the house, let him not come down to take them away. And likewise, he who is in the field let him not turn back. Remember Lot's wife. Whoever

seeks to save his life will lose it and whoever loses his life will preserve it." Luke 17:26-33

My daughter Joy called me, she sounded breathless, "Mom!" she exclaimed, "I wanted to talk to you God has been speaking to me, it is so exciting I wanted to tell you what He said to me."

"Tell me!" I answered her excitedly. "I love hearing what God has to say."

"Well," she started, "Remember when we were talking about the Bethlehem star and wondering what it was about?"

"Yes," I replied. It has been on the news the same star believed to be the star of Bethlehem the planets had lined up just as they had when Jesus had been born. And it hadn't happened since He had been born. We knew it had to mean something, but we didn't know what. We had been discussing it a few days earlier.

"God told me what it meant."

I held my breath in anticipation, but what she said next totally floored me.

"The first time it was for the birth of Jesus," she exclaimed, "the second time it is for Satan."

"Satan," I replied stunned.

"Yes," she began explaining, "You see Satan does not have his own plan he just copies Jesus. He counterfeits what Jesus has done. He is being born into earth. Satan will have his time on earth Jesus had His."

I had noticed the correlation in Revelation how the Anti-Christ has a three-and-a-half-year reign just as Jesus had three and a half years on the earth.

"Mom there is more," she said. "God showed me about the mark of the beast and what it is."

I listened intently as she continued.

"Remember how there were Nephilim on the earth in the days of Noah?"

"Yes," I replied, "Nephilim were giants that were born after fallen angels had taken wives of the women on the earth. They corrupted mankind by intermarrying and creating corrupted beings that had to be destroyed. They were not redeemable. And the Bible says it will be as the days of Noah again, but it seems so incredible."

"But God showed me it, Mom. Satan will tamper with human DNA; in fact, they are already breeding human DNA with animals. It is happening in many countries; this is the plan of Satan. They will mix human DNA with other DNA and make hybrid humans."

"How evil," I said stunned.

"God showed me this thing with the homosexual marriage was a forerunner to the mark of the beast."

"How is that?"

"It was a test, like a trial. Satan got the world to totally go against scripture and accept something that was abominable to God. At first there were hardly any homosexuals and people knew it was wrong. But he got people to accept it and there were more and more of them. Now the government has come out with legislation that violently opposes scripture and much of the church has just accepted it."

I thought of the scripture in Romans.

For this reason, God gave them over to their vile

passions. For even their women exchanged the natural use for what is against nature, Likewise also the men, leaving the natural use of the woman burned in their lust for one another, men with men committing what is shameful, and receiving in themselves the penalty of their error which was due. And even as they did not like to retain God in their knowledge, God gave them over to a debased mind, to do those things which are not fitting; Romans 1:26-28

Then in verse 32 it says, *Who, knowing the righteous judgement of God, that those who practice such things are deserving of death, not only do the same but also approve of those who practice them.*

"Instead of standing up to the tests of the times," I said thinking of this chapter I was working on, "much of the church had just followed the thinking of the times and rejected the truth of scripture."

"Yes, that is right, and not only that, the people that do stand up for the truth are coming under attack and it is only going to get worse." said Joy, "This is an important test. But right now, no one is unredeemable. God is reaching out to homosexuals and loves them, and they can repent and be saved. And that is what Christians are now saying and yet still we are labeled as intolerant and narrow minded. But what is coming, these human hybrids, they will not be redeemable. Can you imagine how much worse it will be when we can't offer hope? We will say these beings are wrong, stay away from them and they have no hope of salvation. If you think we are being labeled intolerant now, can you imagine how intolerant we will seem when we stand against a being and offer no hope? We will really be despised, and the truth will be hard to stand up for."

Joy continued, "God showed me that He would not put a human spirit in these creatures. They are not His creation they are corrupted flesh, Satan's way of perverting God's creation. Usually, God will knit our spirit in with our soul and body in the womb, but God said that He would not allow a human spirit to be knit in with these creatures and that the spirit would return to Him. They would have a body and a soul but the spirit in them would be an evil spirit."

"And God told me that we would be under pressure to accept these creatures, and some would actually feel sorry for them, but we were not to accept this." She continued, "Some will even marry these things and their children will be giants."

"Giants like in the Old Testament," I interjected.

I was thinking of the story of David and Goliath, one of my favorites and one I love to tell my grandchildren. But this time as I thought of it, I shivered. These giants were not a cute little story. They were real and they were horrible. They were fearful and evil, and Satan used them to oppress the people of Israel. The whole Israeli armies of fierce soldiers were absolutely terrified of this evil being, Goliath. Suddenly the bravery of David who slew this evil being, with just a sling and a stone, seemed much greater. We will need to be a fearless and full of faith generation like David, I thought to myself.

"But still, I can't believe people will accept this. It is so evil and horrible like a Frankenstein movie" I said to Joy getting back to our conversation.

"They will come up with cures for diseases with this DNA manipulation and people will say it is good, but it is not it is from Satan."

Then Joy added, "Just as the pressure has become greater and greater to accept homosexuality, the pressure will keep getting greater and greater to accept these evil beings and their tampering of DNA. This is the 'love' generation, the problem is it isn't real love; it is a total acceptance of the profane but a rejection of the truth. But it will get worse; the day will come when the pressure will be for each person to change their own DNA! They will call it evolving to higher form. This will be the mark of the beast! The mark will literally change the DNA of those who take it. They will no longer be human; they will be an unredeemable hybrid and their fate will be sealed. And worse yet this will be forced by the Anti-Christ."

"So that is why there is no repentance for those who take the mark of the beast!" I exclaimed. "They are no longer human. Just as the days of Noah! They will have to be destroyed."

I thought of the verses in Revelation that talked about the mark of the beast.

He causes all, both small and great, rich and poor, free and slave, to receive a mark on their right hand or on their foreheads, and that no one may buy or sell except those who have the mark of the beast, or the number of his name. Revelation 13:16-17

Then a third angel followed them, saying with a loud voice, "If anyone worships the beast and his image, and receives his mark on his forehead or on his hand he himself shall also drink of the wine of the wrath of God, which is poured out full strength into the cup of His indignation. He shall be tormented with fire and with brimstone in the presence of the holy angels and in the presence of the Lamb. And the smoke of their torment ascends forever and ever; and they have no rest day or night, who worship the beast and his image, and whoever receives the mark of his name." Revelation 14: 9-11 Joy interrupted my thoughts, "Mom, the mark of the beast is like a counterfeit of the star of David. Remember how we learned the Star of David is two triangles entwined? One stands for God a triune God reaching down and embracing a triune man."

"Yes," I replied, "It is a beautiful symbol. Through Jesus Christ, we have become united to God body, soul and spirit. And I just heard a minister say that when we become born again our DNA actually changes, we become one with God and we get part of His DNA. We literally become children of God."

"Well, that is what Satan is counterfeiting; he is literally making through the mark of the beast, children of Satan, by changing the DNA of these people and corrupting them through the mark of the beast. The mark will affect the person's body, soul and spirit. It is like a virus. A virus comes in and takes over the cells. The mark will come in their bodies like a virus and take over in their DNA and change them."

"We have to stand up to the tests of the times, even unto death." I said. "We can no longer follow the changing thinking of the world; we have to stay true to the truth of the Word of God. "

"Yes," said Joy, "The tests of the times are getting harder and harder. The day may come when we have to lose our life. We can't be like Lot's wife and look back, if we try to save our life, we will lose it."

As I hung up the phone, I thought of all we had talked about. Our truth can no longer be formed by the popular thinking of the times. It seems hard to believe that people would ever swallow such evil but, in every generation, there have been lies that have taken the people of that era.

But also, in every era there have been those whose thinking doesn't change, those who closely follow Jesus and those whose truth doesn't change because they will not compromise the truth of the Bible. These, although may suffer at the hands of those who do not want the truth, in the end they will be remembered as the ones who stood for truth, and they will be remembered as those who passed the test of their times. We will have to begin passing these tests now if we are going to pass the big ones, like the mark of the beast.

And I saw thrones, and they sat on them, and judgement was committed to them. Then I saw the souls of those of those who had been beheaded for their witness to Jesus and for the word of God, who had not worshipped the beast or his image, and had not received his mark on their foreheads or on their hands. And they lived and reigned with Christ for a thousand years. But the rest of the dead did not live again until the thousand years are finished. This is the first resurrection. Blessed and holy is he who has part in the first resurrection. Over such the second death has no power, but they shall be priests of God and of Christ and shall reign with Him a thousand years.

Revelation 20 :4-6

* author's note- I do believe in the rapture and I hope most of us are out of here. But I want to be prepared for anything in case we have interpreted the time of the rapture incorrectly. And maybe some will read this book after the rapture. Who knows? Let's be prepared.

Chapter Twenty-Four

The Dark Night of the Soul

And when the sixth hour had come there was darkness over the whole land until the ninth hour. And at the ninth hour Jesus cried out in a loud voice saying, "Eloi, Eloi, lama sabachthani?" which is translated "My God, My God why have You forsaken Me?" Mark 15:33-34

Jesus was about to face Hell, as a captive. All the forces of evil had unleashed their fury upon Jesus, and they seemed to be winning. Satan had been trying to kill Jesus since His birth but had failed. He incited Herod against Jesus at the time of His birth.

Herod had every child under the age of two massacred. But Joseph, having been warned by God, had taken Mary and Jesus and escaped to Egypt. Satan had been continually inciting others to kill Jesus; once the people took Him to the top of a hill to throw Him off a cliff, but Jesus walked away unharmed.

Several times the crowd had picked up stones to stone Him. Satan had incited the religious leaders against Jesus, they wanted to kill Him. They tried to trick Him by carefully thought-out entrapping questions, but Jesus's answers outwitted them every time. They were no match for Jesus.

The religious leaders were unsuccessful until now. The tables have turned. Satan finally has Jesus in his hands. He has had Him beaten unmercifully. Jesus has been through a whole night of torture at the hands of the Priests and then the Roman guards. There is Jesus, He is no longer recognizable. His back has been shredded by whips containing nails and glass. His beard had been pulled from His face and His face has already been beaten bloody and swollen. His nose has been broken. Jesus' forehead has been pierced with wicked thorns which have been pressed by evil hands into His flesh, a mock crown. The blood from this crown is streaming down His face. Now he is hanging on a cross, an implement of torture. His hands and feet are pierced by large nails, and His blood is dripping down His body and onto the ground.

This is the way Satan operates. He loves torture, he loves to mock sadistically and cause as much pain as possible, anyone he can get his hands on, even children. But now Satan finally has what he really wants. He has Jesus, the prize of all prizes. He is mutilating Him and torturing Him. Satan can hardly wait to get Jesus into hell, to the very lowest and deepest pit, as far away from the Father as he can get Him. So, he can make sport of Him in front of all his cohorts.

But the Father has seemed to allow this. He has turned His back and Satan is having his way. The fellowship between the Father and Jesus has been broken and Jesus literally dies of a broken heart. Jesus breathes His last breath and all the forces of darkness shriek with glee. They bind Him and imprison Him into the lowest dungeon.

Where is God?

Where is God our Father? He is love, how can He turn His back and allow Satan to have his way? Why is He silent? Does God ever turn His back on us His people and turn a deaf ear to our cries while we are suffering? Does He leave us alone? Is pain and suffering His will?

Life Hurts

It seems we begin this life in suffering. We begin our existence in the womb. We feel safe and warm. But in the fullness of time, our life changes, something happens, birth pains. We get squeezed out of our warm comfortable spot into the birth canal. Suddenly we are pushed out of our comfort zone into a whole new world that is unfamiliar and painful. The light hurts our eyes, we feel the cool air. We open our mouths and scream! Life is painful!

I was extremely broken when God got me when I was fourteen years old. I have talked about it in my other books. Summer didn't exist. She was nobody. At least that was the way it seemed. It is hard to live in this world when you feel like you are nobody. You would just rather not be here. That is what it was like for me. The problem is you have to, so you retreat into a silent shell or a make-believe world, or you take on faux personalities to function.

When I got God when I was fourteen years old, I found a place to run to and feel safe. It was Him. The world was still my enemy, but I had my hiding place, and that was God. I would run to Him. I ran to Him often because I was so small on the inside that just a crossword from someone would totally shut me down. I would get dizzy, the room would spin, the fear inside would overwhelm me, and the tears would start flowing. There was no way to stop them. I would have to get away before the sobbing would start. Wherever I was when someone pressed my fear and rejection button, I would have to get away fast! But now I could run to God. He would be there. His love and comfort would surround me. I would get away and run to Him and I would sob in His invisible arms and literally feel His love comfort me.

I learned that the great big God of this universe had a weak spot, a vulnerable spot, and a spot where I could almost control Him. It was His love for me. I would run to Him in devastation and brokenness and cry out to Him, "Help me, help me, love me, love me!" He would be there. If He wasn't there immediately, like a spoiled child I would demand, "Where are you? I know you love me!" And He would come. And that's the way it was for years. Until one day.

My world had become pretty small. I didn't work. I stayed home with my two small children. For the most part I didn't have to come in contact with people except at church. I liked it that way it was safe.

This particular day my husband was home, so I left the kids with him, and I went to a home fellowship meeting from church. I had gone a couple times before and I usually didn't say much. The man who was teaching had an especially close walk with the Lord which is something that enthralled me, and I loved to hear him talk. That is why I had been going. I was surprised they let him teach because it was one of the elders and his wife who were the leaders, and they didn't particularly like this man who was teaching.

This time at the meeting I said something. I don't remember what I said, but I said something. The wife of the elder didn't like what I said. She was an outspoken type of woman. She let me have it. To a normal person it may have been no big deal, but I wasn't a normal person. In front of the room full of people she chewed me out.

I can't tell you how severe this was to me. All I can compare it to is the movie, Jaws. Think of being in the water with that giant shark, and the terror you would feel. I was the swimmer, and she was Jaws. The terror I felt was overwhelming. I could no longer hear what people were saying. I just concentrated on not crying until I could get out of the door. I focused on the door, getting up and going out the door, getting to my car. I needed to get to God, He would help me. I got to my car as the tears started pouring down my face and then the sobs started. "Why did I come here? Why did I say anything? God help me!!!!!"

I reached out to God just as I always did, knowing He would comfort me. He was my cushion between me and this unsafe, unkind world. It was only because of Him I could stand to be here.

But this day He wasn't there like He usually was. Something was wrong. God wasn't answering. I didn't feel Him. I managed to drive home even though I could barely see through the tears. But God wasn't there. He wasn't comforting me like He normally did. I pulled out the big guns. "I know You love me God." I said twisting His giant arm, I knew His weak spot. I knew I was His weak spot, He loved me. But it didn't work this time. God was gone! He was not comforting me. He had turned His back.

I had to have some relief, I needed help, the world had become a vicious place again and I needed a place to feel safe. This woman and her words were larger than life and I felt I was drowning. God was not there for me as He always had been I thought of my husband, Jim. I needed someone to hold me, to comfort me. I rushed in the door crying and sobbing.

It didn't work, my hysterics only seemed to agitate Jim and he seemed irritated with me too. I laid on my bed holding myself and sobbing to God, to no avail. I thought of my twin sister Carol. She has always understood me; she would help me feel better. I bolted out the door to get to my sister.

My inner person was still calling on God continually, I knew Him, I knew that even if He wouldn't comfort me, He could hear me, I knew He loved me, and it was hurting Him to hear me beg for Him. So, in my heart I was begging and crying and telling Him, "I know You love me!"

I got to my sister, Carol's, and I told her what happened. Now my sister has always been there for me but on this day she was not. I think she said something like, "So what." We have discussed this since then and she can't believe she didn't comfort me. She'd had a lifetime comforting me, but this day she didn't. She had the same sharp edges I had been feeling from my husband. I went home and laid down on my bed and cried until I couldn't cry anymore. I felt confused.

In the days that followed rejection seemed to follow me everywhere I went. I was getting heavy doses of it, and it seemed more than I could take. It was like I was running through a forest of rejection getting scratched and poked by every branch and bush. I couldn't believe God had turned His back on me. I called and I called, and I called on God. I knew he could hear me. I knew even if He wasn't going to answer me, I was making Him miserable too. Things got worse than ever. I was going through more rejection everywhere I went, and I was going through it alone.

Then finally, after about a week, God broke His silence. Suddenly He was there again, and I was standing in an ocean of love. He told me what was going on. He told me He was teaching me to handle rejection. And then He gently told me that He longed to hold me, but He reserved the right to hold my hand instead of holding me and to lead me instead of carrying me and to step aside and let me grow.

Yes, there is a time when God seemingly steps aside and allows us to face our enemies on our own. My time in the safe place of God's womb was over. He was pushing me out and I was feeling alone, and it was painful. This started a period that stretched many years of facing difficult circumstances and situations and people, to help me grow. I had many rough times ahead and one year in particular was the hardest year of my life. A time when every area of my life was shaken. And again, it seemed like another dark night of the soul, a time when evil seemed to triumph. I was going through battle after battle, but this is not something new.

It has happened to Job and Peter, Paul and the disciples, and many others too. But most importantly Jesus faced all of Satan's fury. Let's talk more about these things.

Chapter Twenty-Five

The Dark Night of the Soul,
Part 2
The Ultimate Test

Now there was a day when the sons of God came to present themselves before the Lord, and Satan also came among them. And the Lord said to Satan, "From where did you come?" So, Satan answered the Lord and said, "From going to and fro on the earth and from walking back and forth on it." Then the Lord said to Satan, "Have you considered my servant Job, that there is none like him on the earth, a blameless and upright man, one who fears God and shuns evil?" So, Satan answered the Lord and said, "Does Job fear God for nothing?" "Have You not made a hedge around him, around his household and all that he has on every side? You have blessed the work of his hands, and his possessions have increased in the land. But now, stretch out Your hand and touch all that he has, and he will surely curse You to Your face!" And the Lord said to Satan, "Behold, all that he has is in your power; only do not lay a hand on his person. Job 1:6-12

Job faced the ultimate test. He served God. He loved God and he was perfect before God. He had no sin. God called Job blameless. And yet he went through a horrible test. He lost all of his possessions, his children were killed, and then he lost his health. From head to toe he was covered with horrible painful boils. Job did absolutely nothing to do or cause or deserve any of this! He did not bring this on himself. Satan was behind this; it was all his idea. He approached God and asked permission to do this, and God let him!!!! Have you ever wondered why God would do such a thing? I have. Why, oh why, oh why, would God listen to the devil and allow his own servant Job to go through such pain and misery!!!! I have had some conversations with God about it. I have told Him, "Don't listen to the devil!!!!"

Why?

There has to be a reason and there has to be some sense in here. We KNOW God knows what He is doing, but we don't know what He is doing. Not only is Job suffering his terrible dark night of the soul, God is being silent!!! And Satan is in complete control, or so it seems. What purpose could this have?

But wait a minute. Isn't Jesus in a similar situation? He has been tortured, beaten and crucified, and then sent to hell, while God has turned His back. Jesus is totally righteous, and through no fault of His own, He has suffered tremendous evil against Himself.

All of Satan's fury and sadistic evil has been poured out in full on Jesus, the perfect Son of God. It is the same scenario as Job, Job was innocent, too. Satan believes he has defeated Jesus; he has poured out all his hate and fury and he thinks he has won. But.....he hasn't won. In fact, through this Satan has received a death blow. He has been defeated. Jesus defeated Satan at the cross. Jesus has won the victory in this manner.

It is a strange way to win, and millions do not understand it. It is hard to understand. Something big is gained through Jesus' dark night of the soul. Is there something big gained through Job's? Is there something to be gained through ours?

Yes, this is the ultimate test for Jesus. As He passes it, it becomes His defining work in His life. Jesus has forever and eternally become our Savior. He has defeated Satan through this greatest test He ever faces, this dark night of the soul. He has made huge eternal gains through this victory. But it had seemed for a time, like all was lost. All though this test seemed unthinkably hard, God allowed Satan to pour his full cup of misery out on Jesus. What about Job?   Job went through unthinkable horror at Satan's hands, he too went through a dark night of the soul where Satan seemed to win, and God's back was turned. And yet Job passed this test with flying colors. What did he do?

When Job was told everything he owned was gone

and all of his children were dead, when one messenger after another appeared telling Job of his losses, what did Job do? The Bible tells us that Job tore his robe shaved his head and then fell to the ground and worshiped God. He worshipped God! Can you believe this? He held on to God.

His wife speaking Satan's words to him told him to curse God and die. But Job refused. The Bible tells us in all of this Job did not sin nor charge God with wrong. Job is an exceptional man. This is Job's defining moment in his life. This is what he is famous for. He has obtained a testimony, an eternal testimony. He was tested and tried. Satan poured out all he had on Job and Job held on to his faith in God.

There is a lot to this. After Job's total loss and devastation, he is not only totally restored, his wealth doubles. He started with three thousand camels; he ends up with six thousand camels. He has ten more children. He lives a long-blessed life afterwards. But there is so much more he has gained here than camels. {How many camels do we really need?}

Satan almost had a point when he said to God, "Does Job fear God for nothing? Have You not made a hedge around him, around his household and around all he has on every side?"

Satan wanted to destroy Job, but he couldn't. He couldn't get near Job. Job because of his godliness was totally protected on every side. Job was a very good man, but he was untested. Would he only serve God in the good times? Satan thought so.

God did not give into Satan to satisfy Satan's

curiosity in this matter, or even His own. Although I believe now that Job's faith has been tested, Job's righteousness has increased greatly. Now, Job's love for God is proved; it is not because of his blessings, his protection or anything else he has received from God. Everything Job has is now taken away and Job is in terrible suffering, but it does not affect his relationship with God. Job has a new and greater relationship with God now. He serves God no matter what.

But I also think something even more happened here, something of much greater importance. Job, himself has defeated Satan, on his own. In this area, Job has become the victor. Job has faced Satan and won.

Satan bragged to God that Job would curse God to his face!!!! Job's own wife, while Job was in horrible agony, told Job to curse God and die. But Job worships God instead.

Satan has lost. He caused Job unbelievable agony, but Job refuses to curse God, not only that he falls down and worships God. This is his victory. This is his test, and he has passed.

Job has blazed a trail through a spiritual wilderness. He has become closer to God than anyone of his time. Job has obtained in his sufferings an eternal weight of glory! This was the biggest test of his life, and he has passed with flying colors. He has obtained a testimony of faithfulness. And for every generation after him, he has made us a path, the path of patience and endurance, the path of pleasing God. Like Jesus, he has become a blessing to mankind.

So Where is God?

So where was God during Jesus suffering and during Job's suffering? Does God take our suffering lightly? Does He care what we go through? Remember my story in the last chapter? Remember I turned to God and He was gone?

Remember how I pulled on God in prayer saying over and over again, "I know You Love Me." Even though I was young and an immature Christian I had learned something about God. I had gotten a little glimpse of how much He loved me. I was a manipulator. I thought I could manipulate God, like I did everyone else, because I had found His weakness, me. He loved me. But I couldn't. I knew I was hurting Him. I knew He wanted to comfort me and hold me. What I didn't understand was that He loves me so much, that He allows Himself to be hurt for me. He feels my pain but still He will stand back and let me grow, in His great love He does what is best for me. Even though it is painful.

You see He has great things planned for me. He has an eternal future planned for me that envelopes ions of time, eternity. He has an eternal destiny planned for me that is more glorious than I can possibly imagine. It has to do with ruling and reigning with Him. He is making me into the image of His Son.

Where is God in our suffering? Does He really turn His back on us?

No.

He feels every bit of what we are going through

and more. Our Father's love is beyond what we can imagine; it is beyond what our minds can comprehend. He loves us and He feels what we feel, only greater and more intense, because He is moved by us. But His great big Father's heart will always do what is best for us as painful as it may be, for us and for Him.

We as Parents Suffer, Also

We can only compare it to how we feel about our own children. Even though we are human and don't have the capacity to love like He loves. I remember the feeling I had when each of my children first got their driver's licenses. I wondered if other parents felt like I felt. It was horrible. Every time one of them got to that step I suffered. I knew I had to let them go but I didn't want to. The thought of my child out on the road, driving by themselves in traffic was almost too much for me. For a long time, I didn't rest until they were safely home every night. But I still let them go; it was part of them growing up. I kept asking older people, "Did you feel like this too? Will I ever get over this?"

Or what parent with a sick child does not suffer more because of our love for our child? Would we not in a second be sick for them if we could? Well, how much more than us does God love His children? When you suffer, the heart of God is moved greater than you can possibly realize. We need to always remember God is always doing what we need for our own good! He loves us.

Our Own Tests

We, all of us who are on the path of the high calling in Christ Jesus, may face a dark night of the soul. A time when Satan comes at us with all he has got, and we turn around and God seems to be gone. A time when all our faith doesn't seem to be working. Those around us may tell us to give up, or that we don't have enough faith or somehow, we have brought this on ourselves. A time when we totally stand alone, like Job did, like Jesus did on the cross. A time that may not make sense at all to us until we get to the other side of it. A time when Satan has vowed to God we will fall, and he comes at us with everything he has got. A time when we must defeat Satan for ourselves then we also will deliver another major blow to his evil kingdom, for ourselves and for others, like Jesus did, like Job did.

We must stand. This is the ultimate test. To pass it we may only through gritted teeth be able to whisper, "I know God is good." This could be the defining moment in our life.

Like Job and his test.

Like Joseph, who was tested and tried for many years, a slave, a prisoner.

Like David, who slew Goliath.

Like Shadrach, Meshach and Abednego who faced a furnace,

Like Daniel who faced a lion's den,

Like Jesus who faced a cross.

The dark night of the soul is the ultimate test. It

becomes our defining moment, our testimony. Our Heavenly Father stands back and we face Satan's fury without Him. And we defeat Satan for ourselves, and others. We have obtained a new testimony. We have proved Satan wrong. We won't curse God to His face; we will serve Him; we will worship Him no matter what. We deal the kingdom of darkness a heavy blow. We like Jesus and many before us stand. We defeat our enemy.

Job has finished his test. He is still living; of course, he is with the overcomers in Heaven. You will be able to meet with him someday, to sit and talk with him in heaven. He is one of the most glorious people from earth you will meet there. His countenance is radiant.

But you really don't have to wait until you get to heaven to hear Job speak to you because if you are really quiet you can hear what his testimony is to you, right now.

He is telling you to hold on. He is telling you to do what he did. When everyone is telling you to curse God and die, do the opposite, fall on your face and exclaim, "Blessed be the name of the Lord!" He is telling you the darkness you are now facing will soon be traded for an eternal weight of glory. There is something he wants you to know, and that is GOD IS GOOD! Hold on to that.

Yes, God sometimes stands back and lets us face our enemies. He removes His hedge of protection, and we face our enemy and all of his fury. And it forever changes us, we now take our place with the overcomers, we stand in the great Hall of God with the heroes who have gone before us, with those who have faced their tests and passed them, the tests of life, we are now one of them, we belong with them. And our countenance has changed, we look different! We no longer look the same, we now resemble Jesus!

Chapter Twenty-Six

The Dark Night of the Soul,
Part Three,
The Beauty of Suffering

For it has been granted on behalf of Christ, not only to believe in Him, but also to suffer for His sake, Philippians 1:29

We have talked about Job in the last two chapters, but I want to talk about him again and this time I want to dig deeper. I want to look at his story and really see what it is all about. Job story is recorded in the Bible, so we know it is part of the story of redemption. Nothing is in the Bible by accident. What more can we possibly learn from Job?

Job lived in ancient times. He lived sometime after the flood but before Abraham. He comes in at an interesting time period. We have a huge conflict that is already in motion when Job comes to earth. Satan has successfully executed the fall of man in the Garden of Eden. He has stolen the authority God gave to man from

Adam, and he had hoped that he had stolen mankind also, but he hadn't.

Instead, God tells Satan in the garden, "*Because you have done this, You are more cursed than all the cattle. And more than all the beasts of the field; On your belly you shall go, And you shall eat dust all the days of your life. And I will put enmity between you and the woman, And between your seed and her Seed; He shall bruise your head, and you shall bruise His heel." Genesis 3:14*

Satan had thought he had done a quick work destroying the plan of God from the earth, but he is wrong. God has a plan of redemption for man, and it is coming from the Seed of Eve, {Jesus}. In the garden at the fall of man God lets us and Satan know something is coming, a plan of redemption.

What Satan does next is he goes after the seed of Eve, and tries to annihilate God's plan of redemption, and he almost succeeds. He corrupts Eve's seed.

Fallen angels begin to marry the women of the earth and intermarry on earth corrupting the human DNA and causing corrupted flesh. These unions caused giants to be born called Nephilim, which were evil beings, a spawn of Satan. As they intermarry on the earth the corruption spreads. Not only that, these fallen angels taught men much evil arts and the earth began to be filled with incredible evil. The Bible tells us.

Then the Lord saw that the wickedness of man was great in the earth, and that every intent of the thoughts of his heart was only evil continually. And the Lord was sorry that He has made man on the Earth, and he was grieved in His heart. So, the Lord said, "I will destroy man whom I have created from the face of the earth, both man and beast, creeping thing and birds of the air, for I am sorry that I have made them." Genesis 6:5-7

Satan has again caused God much grief. God is sorry He made man. Satan again believes he will wipe out God's plan. There has never been a being like humans before; we are made in the image of God and Satan hates us and wants to destroy us. And he almost does, again, but God starts over with Noah and his family when he destroyed the earth with a flood and Noah and his family were spared on the ark. Their seed, their DNA was uncorrupted.

This is the world Job now lives in. Mankind has begun again. Job lived somewhere during this time. The Bible tells about Job. *There was a man in the land of Uz, whose name was Job; and that man was blameless and upright, one who feared God and shunned evil. Job 1:1*

And in verse 8 God says to Satan, "*Have you considered My servant Job, that there is none like him on the earth, a blameless and upright man, one who fears God and shuns evil?*"

We can see that up to this point Satan's whole objective has been to ruin mankind and destroy God's plan for us. He has failed two times now but now he comes up with another plan. This time he decides to convince God that there is no reason to redeem mankind. When plan one and two have failed he comes up with plan three. The first two times he went after man, this time Satan wants to convince God to abandon his plan for man on the earth.

Here is Job. He is the most righteous man on the earth. He is blameless and God delights in him. God has shown His delight in Job by blessing him intensely. Job is very wealthy. He has seven sons and three daughters. He has seven thousand sheep, three thousand camels, five hundred yoke of oxen and five hundred female donkeys and a very large household. Job is very happy, and God is very happy.

Satan now comes on the scene. This is plan number three. Satan's plan involves around Job because he is the most righteous man that lives on earth. He taunts God. He tells Him that Job only serves Him because of His blessings. He wants to convince God that mankind is not worth saving, that we only love God when he blesses us. We won't love God without His blessings. He taunts God and tells Him to remove Job's blessings and Job will curse God to His face!!!

Job is a shadow of Christ; he is a pre-shadow. He is representing mankind to God, not only to God but also to Satan. The challenge is that man is not worth saving. The objective is to show God we are worthless and evil and not capable of loving God. The purpose is to abort the plan of redemption. Here is Job, righteous and innocent, representing all of mankind before God.

God loves Job, He delights in Job, but He allows Satan to take everything from Job but his life. Righteous Job takes all the fury of Satan. This is Satan's chance to win, and he pours out his entire wrath on Job and Job's suffering is INTENSE. Job doesn't even know it is coming or why, but Job is crushed under Satan's merciless fury, as God stands back, His great heart heavy with sorrow and God waits.

This is Satan's hour, and he strikes where it hurts, Satan wastes no time, not one but all ten of Job's children are killed in a day. Also, every possession of Job's is stolen. Satan gleefully pours out such misery he is sure of his success. How does Job respond? We are told when Job received this news, he tore his robe and shaved his head and then fell down and worshipped God.

Job is not responding the way Satan wants him to. Next Satan causes Job extreme physical pain. Job lives in agony, extreme agony, but in all this Job does not turn on God. The final thing Job endures is misunderstanding from everyone around him, there is none he can depend on, and he stands alone.

Here are Job's words, *"Naked I came from my mother's womb and naked shall I return there. The Lord gave and the Lord has taken away; blessed be the name of the Lord."* The Bible tells us that Job fell down and worshipped.

In Job's extreme suffering, he has worshipped the Lord! Job is crushed, and he worships!

Job is destroyed and he worships! In the midst of suffering Job worships!

Worship in the Midst of Suffering

Do you remember the woman who washed Jesus' feet with her tears and poured out the perfume on Him?

And when Jesus was in Bethany at the house of Simon the leper, a woman came to Him having an alabaster flask of very costly fragrant oil, and she poured it on his head as He sat at the table. But when his disciples saw it, they were indignant, saying, "Why this waste?" "For this fragrant oil might have been sold for much and given to the poor."

But when Jesus was aware of it, He said to them, "Why do you trouble this woman? For she has done a good work for Me for you have the poor with you always, but me you do not have always. For in pouring this fragrant oil on my body, she did it for my burial. Assuredly I say to you wherever this gospel is preached in the whole world, what this woman has done will also be told as a memorial to her. Matthew26:6-13

Luke 7 :37- 47 And behold, a woman in the city who was a sinner, when she knew Jesus sat at the table in the Pharisees house brought an alabaster flask of fragrant oil, and she stood at his feet behind him weeping; and she began to wash his feet with her tears, and wiped them with the hair of her head: and she kissed His feet and anointed them with the fragrant oil.

Now when the Pharisee who had invited Him, saw this, he spoke to himself, saying, "This man if he were a prophet, would know who and what manner of woman this is who is touching Him, for she is a sinner."

And Jesus answered and said to him, "Simon I have something to say to you." So", he said, "Teacher say it."

There was a certain creditor who had two debtors. One owed five hundred denarii, and the other fifty. And when they had nothing with which to repay, he freely forgave them both. Tell Me therefore which of them will love me more?"

Simon answered and said, "I suppose the one whom he forgave more."

And He said to him, "You have rightly judged."

Then He turned to the woman and said to Simon, "Do you see this woman? I entered your house; you gave Me no water for My feet, but she has washed My feet with her tears and wiped them with the hair of her head. You gave Me no kiss, but this woman has not ceased to kiss My feet since the time I came in. You did not anoint My head with oil, but this woman has anointed My feet with fragrant oil. Therefore, I say to you, her sins which are many are forgiven, for she loved much. But to whom little is forgiven, the same loves little."

This story absolutely touches me to the heart. The Bible tells us this woman was a sinner. I am thinking that might be a nice way of saying a prostitute. This prostitute has managed to invest what she had in an extremely valuable flask of fragrant oil. This is her life savings, and she has invested her wealth in this oil. She is literally spending her life savings by pouring this oil on Jesus. She is pouring out her wealth on Jesus.

Something incredible is happening here. This act is considered unthinkable even to the disciples. They are indignant at the waste.   Something that should last a lifetime was just dumped out…. on Jesus.

They don't see the value of what she did.

This woman is broken, I know she is broken. I know because of the amount of tears that she is crying. Enough tears to wash the feet of Jesus. I am sure His feet were dirty. They walked around on dirt roads in sandals. Jesus had dirty feet. This broken woman is washing his feet with her tears, she is kissing His feet, and she is wiping off his dirty feet with her hair!!

This woman has just given Jesus her all. Yes, she is considered too sinful to bother with and she is thought of as dirt. She is broken but all that she has, she has given to Jesus, her wealth, her tears, her love and worship and she is content to wash the dirt off his feet with her hair.

In her brokenness, she spends herself on Jesus. She values him more highly than this Pharisee that invited him to his house. She values him more highly than even the disciples! Her oil is completely spent but for one purpose, to anoint Jesus, to bring Jesus joy.

She did not waste her oil.

My point is the cost of her worship. Like Job her worship has cost her everything! Job's worship is holy because he has lost everything, but he worships God. This prostitute's worship is holy because she has spent her all to give it. Worship in the midst of brokenness and suffering is the most precious worship of all. Only in suffering can we offer up such a valuable offering, an offering as valuable as the oil in the alabaster flask.

Myrrh

When the wise men came to see Jesus at His birth, they brought Him gifts of gold frankincense and myrrh. The root of the Hebrew word for myrrh means bitter. The bark of the myrrh tree is pierced so that the gum from the tree oozes out. The gum hardens into red drops called tears. Myrrh signifies Jesus bitter suffering for us on the cross. He was pierced for our iniquities. The only way to get the valuable myrrh is for the bark to be pierced, and the red tears come forth from the heart of the tree.

There is a beauty in the suffering of Christ. There is also a beauty in our suffering. The most precious and fragrant worship comes to God from a heart that is pierced. This is costly, this is precious and to pour out this pure fragrant oil onto the Lord, that rises up to Him as a beautiful aroma, is never a waste although it comes at such a great a price. The costliest sacrifices are the most precious.

Touching the Heart of God

I want to quote to you a passage from the book *The Call,* by Rick Joyner. In this passage Rick is seeing God's reaction to worship, from those who are suffering. The first part I will quote will be as the Father observes the suffering of Jesus. First Rick describes the splendor and majesty of the Father as he sees Him in all His glory as all those in heaven are at awe at His majesty. Rick feels that there would be nothing greater than to behold Him and worship Him forever.

Then the Father became intent on one thing. All of heaven seemed to stop and watch. He was beholding the cross. The Son's love for the Father which He continued to express through all of the pain and darkness then coming upon Him touched the Father so deeply that he began to quake. When He did, heaven and earth quaked. When the Father closed His eyes, heaven and earth grew dark. The emotion of the Father was so great that I did not think I could have survived if I had beheld this scene for more than the brief moment that I did.

This is the holiest moment. It had been celebrated for thousands of years before it happened, and it will be celebrated for the rest of eternity. This is a very personal moment; it is a moment of love between the Father and Jesus. It is love that is expressed through extreme suffering. Jesus' sacrifice was done in perfect love, perfect love for the Father and love for us. The price is great, very, very great. It is the kind of love that costs everything. It can't be expressed in words, only emotion, only tears. All of heaven is silent as it looks on. Even the sun and earth respond to this moment. The earth quakes and the sun darkens. The moment is so intense that Rick can only see it for an instant: he feels he would not have been able to contain anymore.

Next Rick is shown a worship service in a little church building on earth. The vision came with the knowledge of everything about all those in the room that he was observing as they worshipped the Lord. They were all experiencing severe trials in their lives. But they were not thinking of their trials or praying about their needs. They were worshipping and praising the Lord. Then Rick saw the joy they were bringing the Father. They had moved the Father so deeply that He wept. Rick says, **Genuine adoration expressed by the most humble believer on earth could cause all of heaven to rejoice, but even more than that, it touches the Father. This is why the angels would rather be given charge over a single believer on the earth than to be given authority over many galaxies of stars.**

I saw Jesus standing next to the Father beholding the joy of the Father as He watched the little prayer meeting, He turned to me and said, "This is why I went to the cross. Giving My Father joy for just one moment would have been worth it all. Your worship can cause him joy every day. Your worship when you are in the midst of difficulties touches Him even more than all the worship of heaven. Here where His glory is seen the angels can't help but to worship. When you worship without seeing His glory in the midst of your trials, that is worship in Spirit and in truth. The Father seeks such worshippers. Do not waste your trials. Worship the Father not for what you will receive, but to bring him joy. You will never be stronger than when you bring Him joy, for the joy of the Lord is your strength."

The Privilege of Suffering

Jesus suffering was so intense and so pure was the

incense of His love and worship that came from his heart as He was pierced, that it was enough to cover the sins of all who had lived up to that time and all who would come after Him. It covers all who will call upon His name, it transcends time. The riches of the cross and all that came from it are so immense it will take eternity for us to contain it.

But there is a privilege we can share with Christ, so holy and so precious that our beings can't begin to understand until we are enlarged in the eons to come. Job did it, the woman with the alabaster flask did it. It is the privilege of suffering. Not just suffering for sufferings sake, but to pour our oil upon the Lord, as Job did and the woman with the alabaster flask.

They were pierced, like the Myrrh tree, and like Jesus. When they were pierced, oil, sweet incense was poured out upon the feet of Jesus. Those that are earthly minded can't perceive it, to them it seems like a waste. But all of heaven watches in awe, as the sweet incense of worship arises from those who are suffering on earth. They stand in awe as they see the joy of the Father. The angels long to be a part, the incense is so pure and so sweet that it attracts the angels and they long to attend the believers who are pierced in heart and yet worship. This is holy ground.

Paul said, "*I now rejoice in my sufferings for you, and fill up all in my flesh what is lacking in the afflictions of Christ, for the sake of His body which is the church.* Colossians 1:24

Paul rejoiced in his sufferings. In order to pass the

test of suffering we have to worship God. Jesus told us in our passage from the book, *The Call,* not to waste our sufferings.

Now let's get back to Job. We don't hear another word from Satan in the book of Job. He is long gone. With all the terrors he put upon Job, he could not get Job to curse God. Job has passed his test. Job has done something precious and wonderful for us all. He has taught us to pass this test, or I should say he has taught us the privilege of suffering.

Chapter Twenty-Seven

The Image of Jesus

But we all, with unveiled face, beholding as in a mirror the glory of the Lord, are being transformed into the same image from glory to glory, just as the Spirit of the Lord. 2 Corinthians 3:18

Our ultimate goal is to be changed into the image of Jesus, to become like Him, to be formed into His image. This is the greatest thing we can attain in this life, to grow closer and closer to Jesus until we radiate Him. Until others see Him in us, and we are transformed into His image. We shine with his brightness, and we radiate His glory. His love shines through us and draws others to Him. To obtain this is to ultimately pass the test of life and achieve the highest calling. All our tests are bringing us to this one goal, to become like Jesus.

We Need to See Him

To become like Jesus we need to come to know

Him. We need to know Him as He really is and not just how we perceive Him. We need to see Him. We need to behold Him with an unveiled face. We need to see Him with the eyes of our spirit, to see the beauty of the Lord and to dwell on His goodness. We stand in awe at the greatness of His love, and we worship Him. And then we begin to change.

We will begin to become what we look at. That what holds our attention will begin to form us into its image, whether it is good or bad. It is time to lay aside the distractions, the things that take our attention away from what is most important. It is time to focus. We need to fix our eyes on Jesus the author and finisher of our faith.

What Are You Looking At?

What have you been looking at? Have you been watching television, movies, or playing video games? Are you addicted to soap operas, pornography, or romance novels? What have you been gazing at, looking at, beholding? It will begin to transform you into its image. These things are from the world and the world's way of thinking and will pull our thinking away from the ways of God. These things can be very enticing, I know. I got sucked in.

Summer Learns a Lesson

I rarely watch television or movies at home, but I work in other people's houses on my job, and I get exposed to things I wouldn't normally watch. About twelve years ago I was on my job as a home health aide, and I was staying with a woman who had just come home from the hospital. She was watching a marathon of her favorite soap opera on cable. After being in her home several days I saw enough of that soap opera to get a little hooked on the story. Well, after I was relieved from caring for that patient, I thought, "I will never see that junk again and it's a good thing."

I had another job I went to every Thursday. I would sit in the afternoons with a lady who had a stroke. I had been going there for several years and I really enjoyed it. My patient's husband wanted the television on for her to watch. I really didn't think my lady could tell if the television was even on or not, but I would flip through the channels and try to find something interesting for her to watch. As I was flipping through the channels one day, I ran across that soap opera that I had seen at the other lady's house. I knew better but I thought, "I just want to see for a second what happened in the story."

So, I watched it for a few minutes just to see what happened. That story was such a pile of filth I soon changed the channel. I was disgusted with myself. But the next Thursday it happened again. I flipped over to that channel just to see what had happened, since the last week. I would get disgusted and decide I would never do that again, so a couple weeks would go by but then I would check again. I knew God wasn't pleased. I felt He told me, "No more."

So, I cut it out, at least for a while. Well, one day I

gave into temptation again and I flipped over to the story. I thought, "I just have to see how this one story turned out, and I will never turn it on again." I knew I was doing something I shouldn't, but I had no idea God would punish me like He did. No sooner had I turned the television to the soap opera when I saw something outside run past the window.

"Was that what I thought it was?" I asked myself, "It looked like a llama!"

Then I heard a thunk and the cable went out on the television. I ran to the window. A llama was in the yard, and it ran into the house and pulled out the cable. The only time I had ever seen a llama was at a petting zoo.

As the llama ran off, I hung my head in shame. I knew I had disobeyed God and he had sent a llama to teach me a lesson. I knew I would never watch that show again or any other soap opera and I never did. But God wasn't done spanking me. I was hoping the incident with the llama would be the end of my spanking, but it wasn't. I was never scheduled to go to that home again; the people switched agencies that week. I never got to go back there again. God was showing me that what I did was a big deal to Him, and I wasn't going to get away with it.

It is important what we see with our eyes and what we hear with our ears. Our spirits have all the same senses that our bodies do. What we see with our physical eyes affects our spiritual eyes and what we hear affects our spiritual ears.

I needed to get this kind of junk out of my life. I now try to stay away from things that distract me from what is most important. I want to focus. I don't need to be pulled into the world's way of thinking; I want to think like God's kingdom. I don't want my emotions tied up unnecessarily. I also had to learn my lesson about reality television, also. I don't need to get all wrapped up emotionally in someone else's life; I have my own life to live! We need to be careful what we are beholding because it will change us for the good or the bad.

How to See Jesus

So how do we focus on someone who is invisible? How do we behold Him so we can be transformed into His image?

First of all, we set the focus of our life on Jesus. It is a decision we make. It is not a small decision, not a whim; it has more importance than a marriage. It is step number one, and it is the big one. You are now seeking His will for your life. You will live where He puts you, marry who He chooses and seek Him for every major decision.

Now we live accordingly. We spend time in prayer, worship and studying His word. We also open our awareness to Him. Knowing He is with us daily. Each day we can expect Him to be with us and communicate with us. Sometimes He may speak to you through another person, sometimes through a coincidence or something that happens to you that day.

I remember one time when my daughter, Joy, was little; sometimes she would not want to go to school. One day she asked to stay home. I prayed about it. The Lord said to tell her that she could stay home but that if she went to school, He had a surprise for her. She changed her mind and went. She was excited about her surprise He had waiting for her. At her school that day they announced they were having a drawing, and one student would win a prize. Joy knew immediately she was going to win, and she did. She knew that was His surprise. Jesus was helping her to go to school. He was becoming real to her on a daily basis.

Seeing Jesus in the Word

Can we really see Jesus in this life? Yes, yes, yes. The Bible tells us if we seek, we will find. There are many ways to seek and find Jesus. Of course, the obvious one is the scripture. Jesus is in every book in the Bible from Genesis to Revelation. Here are just a few glimpses of Him from the Bible.

He is the Creator

The Seed of woman

The sacrificed Son

The Passover Lamb

The Manna from Heaven

The High Priest

The Scapegoat

The Bronze Serpent, He became our sin

A prophet like Moses

The Captain of the Hosts

The Judge

The Kinsman Redeemer

The Son of David

The Rebuilder of the Walls

The Lord Our Shepherd

The Wisdom of God

The Lover and the Bridegroom

The Suffering Servant

The Messiah

The Word

The Miracle Worker

The Image of the Father

The Last Adam

The Fullness of the Godhead

The Soon coming King

The Blessed Hope

Everlasting Love

The Alpha and the Omega

Him who was and is and is to come

King of Kings and Lord of Lords!!!

We see Jesus throughout scripture. The Bible tells His story. The Bible follows His genealogy. Jesus is the Living Word.

With an Unveiled Face

We need to begin to see Jesus with an unveiled face. The veils are there to blind us, they blind us to the glory of Jesus. They are put on us by the spirit of the world. They cause us to believe lies about God. They are strongholds of darkness that blind us and blur His glory and brightness and majesty. We need to begin to deal with the lies and untruths that we have accepted about God and trade them for the pure truth. Then we will begin to unveil our spiritual eyes and the vision of Jesus becomes clearer, His glory becomes brighter. The clearer the image of Jesus we have the more we become like Him.

Do you have veils that are blocking your image of Jesus? Do you believe God is mad at you?

Do you doubt that He loves you?

Do you think you cannot trust Him?

Do you think you are unimportant to Him?

If you said, "yes," you have some veils that need removing.

Or maybe you have some different veils.

Have you made God too small?

Do you think God does not know how you feel or what you are going through?

Do you think He is too busy to be intimately acquainted with everything about you?

Do you think it is difficult for Him to be everyplace at the same time and that includes time? He sees you the day you were born, and he sees you ten thousand years from now, simultaneously, because He is outside of time. Everything in the universe exists because of Him and through Him and by Him; He is the life in you, and He is even the life in His enemies. Have you made God way to small?

Then you have some veils to remove. Or when you think of God do you think of someone else, like an unkind pastor or priest who offended, you in some way, or even a father figure who never loved you and now you think that God is like they are?

Then you have some veils to remove.

Do you blame God for some event that happened, like a death or a sickness and you think God put that on you?

Then you have some veils to remove.

We need to remove the veils that blind us from who God really is. They are cleverly crafted lies from the enemy to keep you away from God. And to keep you from seeing God as He really is. The truth about God is so powerful that just to behold Him will begin to change us into His image.

Removing veils from ourselves can be a

scary thing. It is facing the truth instead of hiding behind a lie. It means the works of darkness we hold onto will have to go.

The Plumb Line

The light from Jesus' face shines brighter the sun. Jesus is pure light, pure truth. His light penetrates through every atom of our being, lighting up every impurity we have hidden in our hearts. To face Jesus in all of His glory even for us who are redeemed is terrifying. I have had this experience once and I thought I was going to die. I felt like my every thought and word and deed was being held up to a giant plumb line and I was very crooked. The plumb line was his purity and light.

In Isaiah chapter 6, Isaiah has a vision of heaven. He sees God sitting on His throne and Isaiah says, "Woe is me for I am undone! Because I am a man of unclean lips, And I dwell in the midst of a people of unclean lips; For my eyes have seen the Lord the King, the Lord of Hosts." Isaiah faced God in all His glory and he felt the same way I did he said he was undone.

Only God is pure, only God is righteous, only God is truth, not until we come into complete agreement with God in everything, will we become straight with His plumb line. We have to let go of each and every lie and untruth we hold to and live by and speak and come into complete agreement with the real truth. We never need to seek God to get our way. We need to seek God to find His way and come into agreement with Him, Truth, and we will begin to change into His image and start to reflect His glory.

The Highest Calling

There are many in the Bible and throughout history that have passed the tests of life with flying colors. They have been faithful, and they have changed the world for the better.

But there is something even higher than that, there is another level that can be attained, a higher purpose and a higher calling. It is one thing to change the world, it is quite another to deeply move the heart of God.

It is the highest calling.

It can be attained by anyone, it was obtained by many of our Bible heroes, but it can also be attained even by those who are unknown. You don't have to be smart or have any special skills. It can be attained by you.

Just desire Him and walk with Him, to gaze on Him and be formed into His image.

It is the Highest Calling. It is to know intimacy with God. It is to become like Christ. It is to be formed into His image. This is the highest test to pass. This is the ultimate goal. This is the highest and final test.

Enoch

Enoch attained the highest calling. Enoch walked with God. Enoch had intimate fellowship with God. The Bible tells in the book of *Genesis, 5:24 And Enoch walked with God; and he was not, for God took him.* And in

Hebrews 11:5 By faith Enoch was taken away so that he did not see death, "and he was not found, because God had taken him," for before he was taken, he had this testimony, that he pleased God.

Enoch made intimacy with God his highest goal. Enoch was so close to God that God just took him to heaven, he never died. Enoch was so close to God that the angels that fell during his time on earth, asked Enoch to intercede with God for them!

Rick Joyner in his excellent book, *The Path,* tells of a prophetic encounter he has with Enoch. I will quote the book as Rick describes Enoch.

I could not help but stare at Enoch. I have never seen anyone so deeply full of love. I have never seen a smile that made you feel so good, so accepted and valued. I just did not expect Enoch to be anything like this-- perhaps the happiest person on earth.

To me this sounds a lot like Jesus. Enoch has such a wonderful happy presence that Rick desires what he has. I am going to quote from the book two passages, in which Enoch tells Rick why he is so happy.

"I was the first to walk with God after Adam. The more I sought Him the more He became my joy. Then the time I spent with Him became more desirable than anything in the world. Just being with Him was on my mind night and day. He became my life."

"What I have is the joy of the Lord," Enoch continued. "This is not a gift but fruit. It is the fruit of walking with the One who is the greatest desire of every heart. The closer you walk with Him the more joy you will

have. The joy that you have in Him then becomes a joy in His people, in His creation and in everything He calls you to do. This is because you will be doing it with Him. Getting closer to Him will change you into who He made you to be. When you get closer to the consuming fire than the warmth of His fire will be in you."

Enoch is telling us something profound and yet something simple. Enoch was perhaps the closest anyone has ever been to God. He has obtained intimacy with God on a much higher level than anyone ever has. It is a love relationship with God, and he has taken on the image of Christ. He exudes love and joy.

Later, after Rick has talked with Enoch, he has a conversation with the prophet Elijah. He notices Elijah's countenance is different from Enoch's. Elijah explains to Rick it is because he did not love others as much as Enoch did. Rick asks Elijah a question and learns from Elijah just how important our choices in our life on earth are.

"You walked with God too, and you were trusted with some of the greatest power He ever revealed through a prophet. Why aren't you as joyful as Enoch?" I inquired.

"I do not mind you asking, and this is important for you to understand. What you become in your life on earth will be who you are forever, without the carnality of course. If anyone on earth realized how much their life on earth impacted their eternity, they would be in pursuit of the fruit of the Spirit more than any treasure or accomplishment.

The greatest treasure of all creation is love. Love

is the foundation of true joy and peace, and the essence of what man is created to be. God is love and if you walk with Him as you are called to, this will be your portion."

This is the secret to the highest calling in God, to pursue God, to walk with Him as Enoch did. We have to do this now in our life on earth. Enoch had done this in greater measure than Elijah and that is why his countenance was more joyful. Elijah then encourages us to pursue the fruit of the Spirit, to pursue the fruit more than any accomplishment.

The fruit of the Spirit is the nature of Christ. *Galatians 5:22*, lists for us the fruit of the Spirit.

But the fruit of the Spirit is love, joy peace, longsuffering, kindness goodness, faithfulness gentleness, self-control.

This is having the image of Christ formed in us, the fruits of the Spirit, His attributes. It is a higher calling, not so much what we do but what we become, that is to become like Jesus.

Chapter Twenty-Eight

Passing the Tests of Life

My Dear Readers,

I hope you are beginning to see things differently. I hope you are looking at your own life which is full of tests, with a new wonder and hope in God, knowing that these tests you are facing are challenges that will lead you higher and farther than you can now possibly imagine. I hope your determination to pass your tests has grown.

I think about Joseph, sitting in that prison for years. He was innocent; he was thrown in prison for something he didn't even do. No one even cared. His father thought he was dead. His brothers had sold him out. Joseph had no natural hope. His last chance was hoping that the Pharaohs butler would help him, but the Pharaoh's butler forgot him. The years went by.

Have years gone by in your life?

I know they did in mine. It seemed like year after year I

went through life with an alcoholic husband and fear. My test was love and forgiveness. My test was facing that giant of fear. There were so many times I looked at my life and thought it was wasted.

I am sure Joseph felt the same way. But he kept passing his tests. I love the story of Joseph; I just love it! Everything changed in one day! In one day, Joseph went from those years of prison to a throne, and wealth and power.

One time the Lord said something funny to me. He knows my favorite story is Cinderella. I have always loved that story. I never get tired of it. It is kind of like Joseph's story. Cinderella is always kind and good and in just one day she goes from a horrible life to becoming a princess.

The Lord told me years ago, in the midst of my seemingly wasted life, "You are the real Cinderella. Everything can change for you in a single day."

I am still wondering why He said that, but my two adorable daughters have heard it their whole lives. When they were little, we always liked princess stories and at night before bedtime and I always told them, "I am the real Cinderella."

I believe God was telling me there is wonderful ending for me and there is. There is for all of us if we keep passing our tests. The hope we have in Him is better than a fairy tale. The Bible tells us the hope we have in Him far exceeds anything we can even imagine.

Joseph faced and passed many tests and so will we.

We have talked about many of them in this book. But we are not alone in this struggle, we have many like

Joseph who have traveled this same road ahead of us and left their torches burning to light our way. The Lord let me talk to Joseph in one of my darkest times. I tell about it in my book, *The Impossible Marriage.* Through that experience I learned something wonderful and amazing. It's something deep in my heart and something hard to describe but I will try.

I learned from Joseph how important each and every one of us is, you and me. This totally blew my mind because I have always felt like the most insignificant person on the earth. But I am not just important to God, I am important to His family, my family, your family.

Joseph and Job and many others in the Bible have run their race and passed their tests, and maybe some in the Bible even failed a few. But they are looking at us now. The Bible talks about it in Hebrews; they are called the great cloud of witnesses. Their focus is on us now, and they want to help us. They want the light they have left us to help us. They want us to pass our tests. And they want us to learn from their mistakes too. They love us and they are cheering us on. They are pointing to Jesus of course but each of them is telling us something, and we need to hear it. We need to pick up our Bibles and read the stories and listen to what they are saying to us.

Joseph is telling us to keep passing our tests no matter what because the end is going to be good! Job is showing us in our suffering to worship. Enoch is telling us the joy of beholding God and walking with Him.

Remember the beginning of this book, nothing we do is done in secret, which includes your suffering and your struggles and your tests. We are standing on a stage of eternal importance and what we do really matters!

I want to remind you one more time what is important. It's not the passing scenes of this life, like my son on the paper route. It is you, the work done in your heart. Remember the real issue is between us and God and it is not really the things and the situations that are so important. The important thing is us and God. We need to reduce it to the simplest form, you and God. Now pass the test.

We want to walk in light and leave behind the darkness.

We want to be faithful in our marriages. We realize our mates fill our biggest need of learning how to love. And yes, we want to learn how to love in our life! When we stand before Him and He asks "Did you learn to love? We will say "YES!"

We want to leave our world a better place than we found it; we will not leave behind any garbage of any kind. Not financial, or physical, emotional or spiritual. We will leave behind blessings on others.

If we fail, we will learn from our failures and continue on. Knowing the biggest thing we can learn from failing is to stop failing. Let's learn obedience and humility.

We are also ready to lay down our lives. We realize that it is something that might have to happen, but we know that there are worse things than dying, so, if need be, we are ready.

We will pass our tests and we will be thankful, remember Merlin Carothers, and his message to us of being thankful in everything. This needs to become a way of life for us. The results are astounding, it works. Remember to regard the weak, be kind to strangers, and forgive those who wrong us. It keeps God's life-giving flow going through us.

We also need to pass the rest test. Where we learn to enter God's rest. When I gave up my struggle with my son, God did more than I could possibly have imagined in a short period of time. That place of rest is a wonderful place to be, remember the Island of Trust. We can face our worst fears and still be at peace.

As we pass these tests, we continue to climb to higher levels. We will keep climbing higher and we will be different, we will not follow popular thinking but cling to God's truth that never changes. This may cost us, but in the end the truth always prevails.

We will even wrestle against our own fleshly soul until we bring it under submission to Christ. Like Jacob we will wrestle, and afterwards we may walk with a limp, but now we no longer walk in our own strength, we rely on God. We are no longer grabbers but princes.

No matter what happens we will remain faithful even if we pass through the dark night of the soul. If so, we will defeat evil for ourselves as Jesus did on the cross. We will take up our own crosses and follow Him faithfully.

And we have learned to value suffering and we do not waste it, knowing the greatest worship is the worship given at the greatest cost, like myrrh, in the midst of suffering. And in our darkest hour, we will as Job did in his darkest moment, fall down on our faces and proclaim,

"Blessed be the name of the Lord."

And don't forget the goal, the aim, and our prize, is to be formed into the image of Christ. To look at Him with an unveiled face and see Him as He really is, in all His glory. And to follow Him closely as Enoch did. To walk with Him, who in Enoch's words is "The One who is the greatest desire of every heart."

Until we look like Jesus, we love like Jesus, and like Jesus we become a light for others. This is truly, to pass the test of life.

With much love,

Your sister in Christ,

Summer

Epilogue

Perhaps you have read this book, but you are unsure of your salvation. If so, we can take care of that right now.

Salvation for your soul is God's plan. He went to great lengths to orchestrate our salvation. There are not several ways to God, only one. The way that God made for you to come to Him, through the sacrificed blood of His Son, Jesus. Anything God does He does right, and your salvation is no exception. As deeply and desperately that you desire God, that is the level He is available to you.

I wanted Him with all my heart! The day I got saved I just hollered "I want God!" That was all it took. He was ready and waiting. I have never been the same; I was born again in that instant. I became a part of God's family. You can too. You can holler or pray; the bottom line is receiving what Jesus has done for you.

Jesus, I need You, please come into my heart and forgive my sins. I receive you today. Amen

Notes

Chapter *2......* *God Calling,* by A.J. Russell, Barbour and Company, Inc. Uhrichsville, OH, page 22

Chapter 8 ...   *Bound to Lose Destined to Win,* by Bishop Earthquake Kelly
Copper Scroll Publishers LLC, Cleveland, Tennessee
page 54

Chapter 9......From, *The Prize Winner of Defiance Ohio*, by Terry Ryan Copyright 2001 Terry Ryan Reprinted with permission of Simon and Schuster, Inc. All rights reserved.

Chapter 10....*Prison to Praise*, by Merlin Carothers
pages83-88
{This wonderful book can be ordered at www.foundationof praise.org.}

Chapter 12.... *How to See in the Spirit*,
By Michael R. Van Vlymen
pages 82-83

Chapter 14...*The Call*, by Rick Joyner, copyright 1999 used by permission www.morningstar ministries.org

Chapter 16....*The Drop Box,* By Brian Ivie, published by David C. Cook

Chapter 19 ....*The Heavens Opened,* by Anna Rountree   Creation House, Lake Mary Florida   pages54-56

Chapter 21....*The Nevertheless Principle,* by Marion Bond West

             Chosen Books pages76-79

Chapter 22...*The Call,* by Rick Joyner copyright 1999 used by permission www.morningstar ministries .org

Chapter 26....*The Path,* By Rick Joyner, copyright 2013

Used by permission www.morningstarministries.org

www.ingramcontent.com/pod-product-compliance
Lightning Source LLC
Chambersburg PA
CBHW031830090426
42741CB00005B/187